ACTIVATE!

POWER UP YOUR BRAND
TO DOMINATE YOUR MARKET,
CRUSH YOUR COMPETITION
& WIN IN THE DIGITAL AGE

BY GAL S. BORENSTEIN

Library of Congress Control Number: 2014949008

CONTENTS

ABOUT THE AUTHOR

Mr. Gal Borenstein is a recognized expert and strategist in digital branding, marketing, social media, advertising, online reputation management and public relations matters. He is the founder and CEO of the Borenstein Group, a top digital marketing communications firm in the Washington, DC metropolitan area that serves clients locally and globally. Since its founding in 1994, the Borenstein Group has helped hundreds of startups, early-stage, growing, and mature companies optimize their brand promise and maximize their brand equity.

Among Borenstein Group's historical clients are trusted brands such as Forrester Research, IntelliDyne, Pragmatics, Aquent, ADT, Airbus North America, National Air Cargo, TCOM, Supreme Group and Learning Tree International.

Borenstein is a vocal advocate for digital engagement across the corporate brand, from the C-Suite to Corporate Marketing to Customer Satisfaction and Employer Branding. Borenstein Group clients benefit from his strategic ability to quickly convert abstract missions into tangible and visible action plans with coherent digital creative and business objectives that serve the client's bottom line. Gal published his first business leadership book **What Really Counts for CEOs** in 2009. Since then, Mr. Borenstein has been featured as a guest commentator on CNN and Fox Business News on strategic marketing and branding issues. In addition, he has been one of the top digital content contributors to influential business leadership social media networks such as LinkedIn, PR Week's The Hub, Advertising Age's BtoB magazine, HR.com, DuctTapeMarketing.com and others.

Gal earned his Bachelor's Degree in Communications from Temple University in Philadelphia, Pennsylvania, and his Master's Degree with Honors in Business and Telecommunications Management from George Mason University in Fairfax, Virginia.

DEDICATION

This book is dedicated to my three sons, **Benjamin, Jacob, and Max,** who help me every day to stay anchored and focused on what really counts and matters in life: family.

Despite my herculean efforts as an educated father to keep up with their innate ability to learn the latest in digital media, every day my sons pointedly teach me how much I don't know. Seeing the world through their eyes continues to inspire me and provide me with a unique sense of parameters that, even as an educated and strategic communication professional, no "book smarts" could.

Max is eleven years old and doesn't know why you'd call someone if you could text them. Jake is fourteen and doesn't know why he'd ever agree to share his digital pics on Facebook, because that's where his parents post their news. And Benjamin, my sixteen-year-old, who is focused on his college aspirations, and already is questioning the veracity of the mainstream media reports on just about everything because his sources on Twitter tend to be more accurate, faster, and provide news in real time.

I also dedicate this book to my wife and life partner, **Dr. Julie Kaplan Borenstein,** a clinical psychologist by trade, who keeps me sane and always loved as I try to juggle too many tasks at once.

PREFACE

What's your reputation worth to you? What's it worth to your clients? What's it worth to your friends? And can you monetize it?

The answer to these questions used to be, "It doesn't matter because it's all about who you know."

Then when business networks of relationships got built, the answer changed to, "It doesn't matter who you know, it's about who knows you."

And then came the Age of Digital. An age where who you know and who knows you doesn't matter as much because your brand is out of your personal control. Through countless mobile devices, it's exposed to anyone with little privacy. Your personal reputation is linked to your company's actions, along with your friends, frenemies, competition, and co-opetition.

With the swipe of a finger on a tablet, or a keystroke on a keyboard, what you do or don't do on Google, LinkedIn, Facebook, and Twitter has the power to either wipe out all that you've worked for, or help you win more business. Online reviews about you as a manager that are posted by your staff can help you attract either the best employees in the industry or the worst C players.

I wrote this book because far too often I meet successful professionals who feel overwhelmed or unsure about how to control and own their digital brands. I wrote this book for those who feel "this too shall pass," because it won't! By transforming the way you view "digital" from "that new technology" to "a powerful business enabler," I believe that you can muster the power to dominate your market, crush your competition, and control your brand destiny.

That's why you need to activate!

TEN THINGS YOU WILL LEARN

1. Why digital engagement is a MUST for your success

2. How to build your digital professional brand

3. How to build your digital corporate brand

4. How to build a culture of digital engagement in your company

5. How to handle social media in corporate settings

6. How to create and sustain online reputation management in the Age of Google

7. How to leverage digital recruitment for better employer branding

8. How to activate marketing automation for growth & more sales leads

9. How to gain a competitive advantage with digital marketing intelligence

10. How to use gamification to engage employees and clients

WHY YOU NEED THIS BOOK

"Believe it or not, the fundamentals of marketing and sales have not changed that much – what's really changed in the digital age is how people buy. Activate! is your road map for mastering how people buy."

– **John Jantsch**
Bestselling Author of *Duct Tape Marketing*
and *Duct Tape Selling*

"Brands of all shapes and sizes must quickly adapt to the digital & social age in order to survive. Read this book to find out how. Now."

– **Dave Kerpen**
New York Times Bestselling Author of
Likeable Social Media and *Likeable Business*

"Anybody who wants to win the future must learn to build their personal and company brand with digital media. With compelling stories and expert guidance, Activate! *provides a blueprint for online success."*

– **Kevin Kruse**
New York Times Bestselling Author,
We: How to Increase Performance and Profits Through Full Engagement,
and Forbes Magazine Leadership columnist.

"Thankfully, you don't need millions of dollars or a huge audience to dominate your industry niche. A little time, a bit of amazing content, and a solid process makes all the difference. This book will show you how."

– **Joe Pulizzi**
Founder, Content Marketing Institute
and Author, *Epic Content Marketing*

"*In* Activate!*, you get the best of two worlds as Gal Borenstein fuses the unchanging best practices of traditional marketing with strategies specifically tailored to the ever-changing realities of the social media. Every page has practical brand-building ramifications.*"

– Richard Levick
Richard is a global PR thought leader and CEO of LEVICK, a global strategic communications firm, and co-authored books including, *The Communicators: Leadership in the Age of Crisis;* and *Stop the Presses: The Crisis and Litigation PR Desk Reference.*

"Activate! *is a call to digital arms – and just what many leaders need to win in today's evolving, competitive landscape. A true digital warrior and champion of established and emerging leaders, Gal Borenstein presents not just 'what you need to know' but 'why you need to do it now,' in one quick read. This book will give you the courage to embrace the digital groundswell and successfully establish your brand. Do so now; before someone else defines you!*"

– Cary Hatch
CEO, Brand Advocate of MDB Communications,
Named to "POWER 100"– WBJ, Washington, DC

"*Creativity can no longer be ignored as the key success factor for sustaining strategic advantage. Yet few know what or how to make it happen. This book wakes us up to the importance of digital branding in this innovative journey, and the tools for getting it done.*"

– Don Schmincke
Author/Speaker/co-Founder, *Creative IQ*

"In today's fast paced business world, smart marketing is often the only difference between knock-out success or just being ignored. Activate! will give you the inside track on building a business exploding with impact. Gal weaves witty anecdotes and smart storytelling around solid marketing strategy that you need to take action on right now."

– Dan Waldschmidt
Bestselling Author of *EDGY Conversations*

"In a world heavily dominated by digital media and communications, building key relationships and your personal brand continue to be important components of achieving success. Gal's book provides keen insight and guidance on how to build and manage your digital brand and key relationships that allow you to drive the desired results."

– Sid Fuchs
President & CEO, MacAulay-Brown, Inc.,
and author, *Get Off the Bench*

INTRODUCTION

Imagine a leader. He or she is a CEO or a president or a king.

The leader receives a communication.

In ancient times, this communication could only have come from another human source: a messenger or colleague. In 490 BCE, Pheidippides, the famous Greek messenger, ran from the battlefield of Marathon to Athens to announce that the Persians had been defeated in the Battle of Marathon. Upon delivering his good news, he collapsed and died.

Fortunately, since that time we humans have made tremendous progress in communications technology.

By the Middle Ages, a man on horseback could deliver a handwritten message on parchment. An amazing improvement!

Then in 1445, Johannes Gutenberg invented the printing press. Identical documents could be printed and distributed in large quantities.

In 1832 came the telegraph, the first electronic messaging system that permitted the instantaneous transmission of information over long distances.

Alexander Graham Bell gave us the telephone in 1876, and the human voice could be transmitted in real time. Then came radio and television.

As technology progressed, successful businesses embraced each new possibility. After all, in business, the only constant is change. If your business is static, you'll quickly lose ground and be overtaken by your rivals. That's the beauty of our free market system: every company, CEO, and stakeholder has a powerful incentive to embrace change, improve, and move ahead.

Today, we're in the middle of another great leap in technology—the digital revolution. It's happening right now. You and I are experiencing a period in history as important as when Gutenberg invented his printing press, or Bell invented the telephone. We are witnesses—and participants of history.

The name of this book is *Activate! How to Power Up Your Brand to Dominate Your Market, Crush the Competition, and Win in the Digital Age.* The word "activate" has been chosen carefully. It means to energize, to infuse with vitality. It's kinetic, not static. It's like life itself. You can activate your company or organization by leveraging the new wave of communications technology—digital engagement. By doing so, you'll stay at the forefront of the very best business practices. You'll have confidence in knowing that you won't be easily overtaken.

Communications is at the heart of every enterprise. It's essential both internally and externally. The stakeholders of an organization—board, staff, vendors, consultants—need real-time, comprehensive communications about relevant events happening both inside the organization and outside in the marketplace. Data overload is undesirable; precision, speed and accuracy are essential.

The digital revolution is changing the standards for communications. What was acceptable twenty years ago is now unacceptable.

The goal of this book is to introduce you to the vast potential of the digital era and to de-mystify many of the concepts that you may have heard of. I'll talk about ideas that are both cutting-edge and practices that have quickly become ubiquitous.

The book starts with a fable. Our hero, Emperor Ceo, is a likable enough monarch who tries his best to do the right thing. I'll show you how the emperor learns about new ideas and the consequences of clinging to the old ways. I'll reveal the keys to your corporate brand, discuss generational issues, delve into marketing automation, shine a light on reputation management, and much more.

We'll see how marketing has become a two-way street. Gone are the days when one-way advertising was your only choice. Today, your customers both talk back at you and talk about you and your brand. The market has become an electronic town square where everyone comes together to share opinions. Even your employees talk about their experiences working for your company. Prospective hires are walking in your door armed with a set of opinions that they've found on the Internet. You can't stop it. That's just the way it is. This book is designed to help you stay one step ahead of the crowd, and to ride the wave of the digital revolution instead of being swept under.

As an added value, I've included the exclusive personal reflections of a select group of leaders in our industry. You'll discover their views in the "Insights" sections throughout the book. These experts offer real-world experiences that can help you understand and master the changes that are sweeping across your marketplace. I'm very grateful for their keen observations and personal perspectives that have added richness to our conversation.

Ready? Let's get started!

CHAPTER 1
THE DAWN OF SOCIAL LISTENING

Long ago in a kingdom far away, there lived an emperor. He was very vain, and wanted nothing more than to wear the finest and most expensive clothes.

(I know you've heard this tale before. Bear with me—there's a new twist.)

Emperor Ceo, as we'll call him, ran a tight ship. His princes deferred to him, his soldiers saluted him, and his subjects bowed when he passed by. He loved to issue orders, which he expected to be obeyed without question. No one in his kingdom dared to say a contrary word. Indeed, Emperor Ceo lived in an actual ivory tower (this was before the trade in ivory had been outlawed), and from the high windows he enjoyed looking out over his vast holdings and watching his subjects as they went about their daily tasks. Every week he would issue a new commandment. Each commandment was laboriously carved onto a set of stone tablets, and these were distributed to all the villages in the kingdom, where they were set up in the public squares for all to read. There was no method of reply; that is, no stone tablets were ever sent back to the ivory tower. It was a one-way system, which Emperor Ceo liked just fine. He issued edicts, and his subjects listened.

You know the story. One day Emperor Ceo hired two swindlers who promised him the finest and most regal suit of clothes. The fabric to be used was so exalted that it could not be seen by anyone who was either unfit for his position or was hopelessly stupid. As soon as Emperor Ceo endorsed the project, these swindlers—Slick & Shark—began their work. They set up a state-of-the-art workshop that appeared to be busy with activity. Of course, no one in the castle could see the fabric that Slick & Shark were allegedly using, but no one said anything. It was not their place to do so, and there was no forum for open discussion.

After collecting their fat fee and making a show of working diligently, the swindlers reported that the costume was finished. They pretended to dress Emperor Ceo, who then proudly marched in procession before his subjects. The townsfolk played along with the pretense, not wanting to appear stupid or unfit for their positions. Then a child in the crowd, too young to understand the advantages of keeping up the pretense, blurted out that the emperor was wearing nothing at all. In short order, Emperor Ceo was disgraced. The value of the kingdom's stock plummeted on the exchange, gloom fell over the land, and many of his subjects lost their jobs.

The entire affair was an unmitigated disaster.

Did it have to end this way? No.

Let's fast forward a few centuries to the modern era and retell the story.

In our retelling, Slick & Shark were hired to create a line of clothing for Emperor Ceo and his kingdom. After working on their project for a few weeks, they presented their clothing line to Emperor Ceo.

Immediately one of the pages in the court tweeted, "Problem with #Slick&Shark wardrobe. Fabric seems invisible. Emperor Ceo is unaware."

Another page posted on her Facebook account, "What's up w/Slick & Shark vendors? Anybody know their qualifications? Clothing is hard to see."

A courtier tweeted in reply, "#Slick&Shark are known for scams. Big problems w/supply chain in the neighboring kingdom. Bad reports."

One of the court attendants tried to find the Slick & Shark LinkedIn account. They had no LinkedIn account! She sent a frantic email blast to the Wardrobe Division. "Has anyone done due diligence on Slick & Shark? We need to get ahead of this issue and avoid a shareholder revolt. Get the project manager into a meeting pronto."

Then word leaked out to the public. The kingdom's Facebook manager reported an increasing number of comments on the kingdom's page. Here's one: "Clothing in the kingdom is a joke. Whoever designed the Slick & Shark line needs to have their head examined. Weird transparent threads are not worth the money!"

Another villager posted, "Slick & Shark are more like Dumb & Dumber. The kingdom ought to dump these losers pronto and get back to quality products."

Here's another one: "Slick & Shark? Please. Don't waste your money. Clothing so flimsy it seems like it's not even there! Cheap and shoddy."

In his office, Emperor Ceo checked on his computer dashboard, which displayed not only the kingdom's key performance indicators in real time, but also the social media digest of the day. To his horror he saw the digital uproar over Slick & Shark. The members of his court, the workers in the kingdom, the consumers in the villages—they were all were engaged in a spirited discussion of the Slick & Shark wardrobe project, and the feedback was universally bad.

The Slick & Shark project was in big trouble. To continue it without major changes would mean disaster.

Emperor Ceo summoned Slick & Shark to the throne room, and demanded an explanation.

If it would make you feel better to hear that the two swindlers repented and dedicated themselves to producing quality clothing for the emperor, fine. In the retelling that I like, they got their heads chopped off.

However, the outcome and moral of this little tale is that in the old version, the kingdom suffered greatly. The emperor was disgraced, and people in the villages lost their jobs. In the new version, there was some short-term pain. It was not necessarily fun for the emperor to read negative comments from his subjects on the kingdom's Facebook page. But Emperor Ceo knew that these negative comments were a priceless gift. The explosion of incredulous tweets was a good thing. The exposure of Slick & Shark as swindlers could not have come too soon. The openness of the kingdom, and the environment in which everyone, even the part-time pages, felt empowered to question the status quo, made it possible for a wayward project to be salvaged before it did any real damage.

Compared to the orderly existence of the old kingdom, the new process of social listening was messy. Information now flowed up, down, and sideways. By contrast, in the old kingdom, the flow of information went one way: from the emperor out to his empire. The path was neat, tidy, and unidirectional. The result of this rigidity was that the Emperor lived in a surreal bubble that did not correspond to reality.

There's an all-encompassing word for the actions that the emperor's new kingdom—and indeed any enterprise—needs to take to enhance its competitive ability and remain ahead of the pack. That word is *activate*. It means to both create and energize the digital tools that will carry it forward. It refers to the entire spectrum of digital culture. It means to embrace the new and discard the stagnant status quo, like a butterfly sheds its useless old cocoon and spreads its wings in flight.

THE HIGH COST OF LIVING IN AN IVORY TOWER

The story of Emperor Ceo may be a fable, but in real life the failure to activate leads to conditions that can be stark and painful. You know what I'm talking about: General Motors, for starters. For nearly forty years—from the nineteen seventies until its bankruptcy in 2008—the once-mighty GM resembled a bloated dinosaur whose behavior mirrored the kingdom of Emperor Ceo. The company insulated itself. Divisions and departments were siloed. Customer opinions didn't matter. Innovation was stifled. The "yes-men" were promoted and coddled. Directives were sent from management to the front lines, and information never flowed the other way around. There was very little listening, social or otherwise.

The behavior of managers was so disconnected from reality that two new terms had to be invented to describe it:

The GM Nod. This was a practice of GM managers sitting in a room, nodding in agreement at steps that needed to be taken, then leaving the room and doing nothing.

The GM Salute. This was the habit of employees going through meetings, with their arms folded and pointing outward at others as if to say that the responsibility lay with them, not with themselves.

Meanwhile, companies like Toyota and even lowly Volkswagen were increasing their global market share by relentlessly pursuing quality and responding to consumers.

As it emerged from bankruptcy and returned to profitability, GM and its new CEO Mary Barra found themselves faced with a nightmare that no company wants: paying for deaths caused by defective products that were made years ago when different executives ran the company. These lethal product failures—most notably an ignition key assembly that could malfunction because of a single part that cost a measly one dollar to replace—were the direct results of the Emperor Ceo syndrome. In the old GM kingdom, you kept your mouth shut and collected your paycheck. When the emperor passed by, you smiled and waved.

By now, I suppose you're ready to remind me that this book is supposed to be about the wonders of digital communication, and how it can transform a company. It is. Imagine, for a moment, if during the past forty years that GM had been activated. What if it had a robust Facebook page, where there had been an open and inclusive forum for discussing the company and its products? What if the company had a vice president of social media who had the clout in the executive suite? What if Emperor Ceo had been willing to listen to feedback from his engineers, sales staff, and consumer advocates? What if networked dashboards had provided real-time reports of defects to every stakeholder? The tragedies of fatal product failures might have been avoided.

As we go forward in the book, here's the thing that I hope you'll understand: digital culture is just another tool, but it's a really good one that you'd better add to your toolkit.

Here's an example of how it's a tool, just like any other tool. Say you've got two people—Mary and John—who are each building a house. They've each got lumber and saws and concrete. They each have a set of plans. Both of them are skilled builders.

The only difference is that Mary has a hammer. Not a fancy contraption, just an ordinary hammer.

John has no hammer. He's got nails, but no hammer. Not even a rock to use as a substitute.

Who do you think is going to be able to build a house, on time and on budget? Mary, obviously. I feel sorry for poor John. He's going to have a very difficult time competing with Mary. He may be just as smart as Mary and just as well intentioned, but not having a hammer puts him at a serious disadvantage.

In today's competitive business environment, digital culture is a tool that has become as ubiquitous as a hammer. You need it in your organizational toolbox, and you need to know how to use it.

FACTS YOU NEED TO KNOW

▶ The reach of online media such as blogs and social media sites reach almost 80% of active U.S. Internet users today, a number that exceeds 245 million people.

▶ The growth of online media today is so rapid that by 2020 over 75 billion devices will have access to the internet.

▶ "50% of all companies are on their way to the cloud and one billion smart phones will be in use globally by 2016."

CHAPTER 2
THE DIGITAL CORPORATE CULTURE

In our little fable that I related in the first chapter of this book, Emperor Ceo's old kingdom may have been many things, but it was not a digital culture.

What does this mean – "digital culture?" It sounds like some kind of high-tech yogurt.

When I say digital culture, I'm talking about two different yet closely related aspects of an organization's operations and structure.

One is technological—the physical tools that we humans have at our disposal.

Since the end of the twentieth century, the world has seen digital technology explode from being a laboratory oddity to a ubiquitous part of everyday life. As digital technology has steadily improved, people, in their endless inventiveness, have found ways to create digital networks for sharing ideas, information, and cute kitten videos with their friends, family, and colleagues worldwide.

We've come a long way. Personal computers were unknown in the 1980s. Today, there is more computing power in your smartphone than there was in any of the Apollo missions that flew to the moon.

The Internet, which first took seed in the late 1950s, emerged by the mid-1990s as a global force for digital communications. It was not long before big companies developed intranets for communicating within the organization, as well as extranets that were accessible to non-employees such as vendors and customers.

The first emails were sent in the late 1970s. An estimated 150 billion of them are now sent every day.

Telephones have been freed from their copper wires and have gone fully mobile. According to the International Telecommunication Union, in the world today there are roughly seven billion mobile phone accounts, which serve 95.5 percent of the world's population. It's an impressive market penetration; in 1990, this number was close to zero, while less than a quarter-century later nearly every human being on the planet has access to a mobile phone.

Facebook was founded in 2004, and ten years later could claim 1.23 billion monthly active users, 945 million mobile users, and 757 million daily users.

YouTube went "on the air" in 2005. By 2014, the video service attracted more than one billion unique users each month, while over six billion hours of video were watched each month.

Twitter was hatched in 2006 (sometimes you can't imagine how people managed to survive in the Dark Ages before Twitter), and by 2014, boasted 225 million monthly active users who were busy tweeting their 140-character messages.

The last but not least of our Big Four social media giants, the professional networking service LinkedIn was launched in 2003, and after a period of slow growth mushroomed to an estimated 300 million users.

If for some reason you're not up to speed on them, any fifth-grader will give you a complete tutorial on these services.

In addition, the digital universe includes a wealth of tools that form the invisible fabric of any competitive enterprise. These include networked computer dashboards that can present a set of key performance indicators in real time to every stakeholder from the CEO to the lab technician in R&D. Everyone gets the same information instantly, facilitating consensus and quick response. Documents can be written and edited online, with every iteration recorded. And when you're on the road, your desktop can be sent to your smartphone.

What this means is that your communications toolbox now has many more tools than it did in recent history. This is one aspect of the digital culture.

The other aspect is how people use these tools.

Let's be honest. During the thousands of years that humans have done business with each other, some organizations have been agile in their communications—both external and inter-nal—while others have not. In ancient times, couriers ran with messages, like Pheidippides, who in 490 BC ran twenty-six miles from the battlefield of Marathon to Athens to announce that the Persians had been defeated. Leaders sent memos on parchment or paper, or hoisted flags on the masts of their ships, or sent Morse code signals. Somehow, progress was made. The Pyramids got built without Facebook. Columbus sailed to America without tweeting his daily experiences. We managed to land a man on the Moon without the astronauts being on LinkedIn. Things got done; maybe not very efficiently, but they got done.

What the digital culture creates is an environment where communication can be done much more *quickly, easily, and cheaply,* but *only if you choose to use the tools.*

Today, you can have Company A, which is fully activated both internally and externally because it uses every available digital tool, and across town you can have its competitor, Company B, which does not leverage these tools and instead lives in a world like Emperor Ceo. One company has a digital culture, one does not. One company is engaged in social listening while the other clings to the old one-way-street approach. One company is light and agile, while the other is heavy and brittle.

Everyone is entitled to their opinion, but I would not want to bet on Company B to last very long. In today's economy, the stakes are too high and the competition is too intense. With the first shift in public taste, or a threat from a new competitor, or a downturn in the economy, Company B will sink like a rock.

Online marketing has transformed how organizations interact with their customers and prospects. Interactive and affordable, it encompasses a wide range of digital marketing tools including email marketing, blogs, social media marketing, e-newsletters, video marketing, SEO, and much more. Rapidly changing and complex, it can play a critical role in keeping the company's sales robust during both good and bad times.

Today, online marketing encompasses three types of interactions: distributing a message in various digital formats (email newsletters, websites, online promotional videos, tweets); listening to the responses from consumers, and *participating* in the discussions that consumers have with each other.

This third activity—participation in public forums that the company does not directly control—is something that is totally new in the emerging digital culture. In the old days, distributing your message was standard procedure. You bought ads on TV and sent junk mail to people on lists. Today, there's still plenty of this old-school one-way marketing going on. For the 2014 Super Bowl, for example, advertisers paid an average of four million dollars for each thirty-second commercial. In the 2012 presidential election, television advertising spending reached a total estimate of nearly one billion dollars. Make no mistake—one-way advertising is still big business!

As for the flow of information back to management—listening—in the old days companies made crude efforts to collect feedback from both employees and consumers. On the wall outside the manager's office, employees might have found the old-school "suggestion box," where they could place their ideas. As for consumers, you could always call the customer service line and complain to the hapless phone operator, who may or may not have any influence over management decisions about the crummy product you just bought. The digital culture has transformed this process, making it much easier for consumers to contact a company and voice their opinion. (Whether—and how—the company chooses to respond is another story.)

With the advent of digital communications, what has been truly revolutionary is an organization's ability to participate in the flow of opinion and information that swirls around in the digital universe. It's like being in the digital town square on a busy afternoon when everyone's out and having conversations, and you're right in the middle of it.

This participation is becoming increasingly mandatory. Digital culture has relevance to every business owner because whether you like it or not, the people who are busy Facebooking and tweeting and posting YouTube videos are your customers. They are talking to each other in the digital town square and gossiping over digital backyard fences, and it's very likely that they are talking about your company or your product. As a business owner, you can choose to either ignore the conversation and hope that it doesn't affect you, or become engaged in the conversation and learn from it.

As we saw in the fable of Emperor Ceo, the first place that digital communication should be taking place is within the company itself. Leaders need to understand that the traditional metrics of business qualifications—the MBA, or years of inside management experience—no longer guarantee success. In the pre-digital world, corporate experience trumped knowledge. In the new world, digital knowledge can often trump corporate experience.

Just take a look at who's at the top of the list of richest and most inspiring CEOs, and you will find younger faces, many age forty or under, like Facebook's Mark Zuckerberg, Under Armour's CEO Kevin Plank, Google's CEO Larry Page, Groupon's CEO Andrew Mason, and many more.

What do they all share in common? They think like digital leaders. Without decades of business experience, they adroitly applied digital knowledge to their branding, marketing, and advertising in an innovative and disruptive way that leap-frogged what most industrial boardrooms are able to accomplish in traditional corporate ideation cultures.

Contrary to common belief, digital leaders aren't just creating "digital businesses." They apply their knowledge acquisition and entrepreneurial zeal using digital techniques that help their bricks-and-mortar businesses grow. Just look at non-digital companies like Virgin, Under Armour, Generac, and Tesla Motors. Simply put, these leaders aren't exclusively online companies, yet they are very much plugged into the digital marketplace.

Will your business survive if it remains non-digital? Will your company survive if your leaders don't become digitally inclined?

A COMPANY'S LEVEL OF DIGITAL READINESS

In my experience as a strategic branding professional, by using some of the following behavioristics to make observations, I can identify a company's level of digital readiness (or lack thereof). Here are some of the key metrics that indicate that an organization is not yet embracing the digital corporate culture—and needs to activate or risk being left in the dust.

▸ Management learning and insights are obtained only from internal resources. This is the echo chamber effect, where internal opinions are repeated so often that they become accepted as fact. Actual evidence from the marketplace is ignored or discounted.

▸ Management culture prohibits or ignores interaction on social media. The culture is one of fear that employees will say stupid things or somehow fail to tow the party line.

▸ Senior management thinks that its client list is proprietary, even though it is to be found in any Google search. People out in the marketplace often know much more than you think they do—and they love to talk about it.

▸ Inside the big gleaming office tower, you cannot spot an iPad unless you're in the Millennials section of the cubical farm. The folks in the corner offices think, "The kids have these crazy things they do… but around here, we do serious business. We've got no time for social media nonsense."

▸ To appear informed, the CEO is using a tablet only to check his or her emails. But this is just another way of keeping your head in the echo chamber.

Are these metrics shallow? Could they be misleading? Maybe. But so is the suit and tie from a high-end boutique and the Bentley. Culture is driven by the behavior of leadership.

Digital readiness is not cosmetic. Change doesn't come from Emperor Ceo opening a Twitter account and having his admin assistant post inane tweets about his daily activities. Digital readiness comes from adopting a new outlook from the top down. Growth is powered by efficient and effective organizational structures and cultures. The way that companies embrace digital culture matters as much as whether they do it at all.

The components of a digital culture that businesses must adopt include agility, collaboration, empowerment, and a sharp focus on the customer. Organizations with an organic digital culture are far more adept at disrupting business models and industries. They respond to change more quickly, and a continuing focus on data and their customers keeps them in front of the pack.

Activated companies know that they cannot maintain their advantage by sitting on cash cows. They strive to adopt disruptive players' collaborative strategies, agility, and customer focus. As digital technology promotes rapid changes in costs, revenues, and customer behavior, no company can afford to stick with the status quo.

Across all sectors, businesses that welcome and empower the potential of digital communications at every level—starting with the ranks of senior managers and the board, and moving throughout the organization—will see digital not as a hurdle, but as the fast track to remaining on top.

FACTS YOU NEED TO KNOW

▸ **Social Media Websites such as LinkedIn, Twitter, and Facebook are becoming favorites by businesses looking to distribute content effectively.**

▸ **"Customers who engage with companies spend 20-40% more money with those companies than other customers."**

CHAPTER 3
THE DIGITAL CORPORATE BRAND

Everyone knows what a "brand" is. It's Coke, or Pepsi, or Apple, or McDonald's. The word can be applied to single products ("Which brand of toothpaste do you prefer—Crest or Colgate?") or to an entire company ("The Toyota brand took a hit after the problem with stuck accelerators led to a massive recall"). It's that simple word or image that provides an easy handle for consumers and investors to identify a company or product. Brands are quickly differentiated by their packaging, logos, prices, and other features. Individual brands are rarely all things to all people. Usually the mention of a brand conjures a defined range of responses, such as "expensive," "cheap," "durable," "throwaway," or "the one that LeBron James endorses."

What then is a digital corporate brand?

As you'll recall, in the previous chapter of this book I made it clear that whether you like it or not, the people who are busy Facebooking and tweeting and posting YouTube videos are your customers. They are talking to each other in the digital town square, and it's likely that they are talking about your company or your product. This activity is external. In addition, your company should have a robust internal digital communications structure, simply because it will help you get more stuff done more quickly, and you'll have a better chance of avoiding disastrous product rollouts like the one suffered by Emperor Ceo.

Taken together, what happens in the internal and external digital town squares constitutes your digital brand.

Your company or organization has a digital brand. Right now, this very minute.

You might say, "Hey, wait a minute! We don't have a Facebook page. We don't tweet. We don't do any of that stuff. Therefore, we don't have a digital brand."

But you do, because your customers are creating one for you.

Here's an example.

Walt Disney World in Lake Buena Vista, Florida is the most visited vacation resort in the world, with an attendance of 52.5 million patrons annually. The complex consists of four theme parks, themed hotels, and an abundance of shopping, entertainment and recreation areas.

Lots of people love going there, and the reputation of Disney is just about as good as you can get. I'm not citing them to be critical, but to tell you that no matter who you are, you have a digital brand that exists online.

There's a website called Disney-world.pissedconsumer.com. It's a site where unhappy pilgrims to the Magic Kingdom can vent their venom for all the world to see. Here's one (edited for clarity):

"Waiting at the Princess Hall to see the characters from Frozen was over four hours...Disney is supposed to be a time of magic, not to wait over four hours.... It has been a waste of time and money... Definitely it was an unforgettable and horrible time here at Disney."

Here's another zinger:

"Many Disney cast members are just really crazy people. You'd think they would behave like employees of a company, but instead, most are on major power trips looking to hurt, insult, control, or abuse guests at Disney. These days most cast members

I encounter are just psychotic, angry, mean, and rude."

Wow! Someone didn't get their dose of magic dust from Tinkerbell, that's for sure.

Will any of these complaints damage Disney or deter visitors? Maybe not, and companies are getting used to seeing online broadsides from either unhappy consumers or just plain crazy people. The point is that all of this chatter—the good and the bad—becomes part of your digital brand.

Your digital brand is also formed by your website, your consumer interface (if you sell to consumers online), your YouTube presence, and everything else that represents your company, good or bad, online.

I know a lawyer—call him "Joe Smith"—who is a perfectly nice guy with a one-man practice specializing in personal injury cases. Unfortunately, Smith was very slow to build up his online presence—he had a crummy website, no blogs, and no YouTube videos. Also equally unfortunate was the fact that Smith got himself disbarred for a year because his legal assistant had commingled some client funds that were being held in escrow (in the lawyer business, this is a big no-no). Once his license was restored, Smith was back in business. Everything was fine except for one big problem: when you Googled his name, the very first result at the top of the page was the screaming headline, "State Supreme Court Suspends Attorney Joe Smith…"

Needless to say, Attorney Smith's digital brand was toxic and needed immediate help. He went to work on his brand, engaged the digital town square, and soon had counterbalanced that bad search result.

CUSTOMER DISSATISFACTION = OPPORTUNITY!

One of the lessons that I'm going to repeat endlessly is that in the digital marketplace, people are going to talk about your brand. They will talk about it whether you want them to or not. They will say good things and bad things. To ignore the chatter is not an option. You need to *manage* it.

This is a true story. Daniel, one of my business buddies, is the CEO of a tech startup that has developed a cool new navigation app. The app combines a calendar, scheduler, road maps, and real-time traffic information to help drivers avoid traffic jams and unforeseen delays. It's a powerful tool that goes far beyond ordinary turn-by-turn navigation apps. Because of the huge amount of real-time data the app uses, the company has to charge a small monthly subscriber fee of five bucks a month.

Recently, a user posted this comment on the company's website. I am reprinting it here verbatim:

Null

Your app is the most promising piece of shit ever. I am using the term piece of shit because it is just a piece of shit right now. -no routes -no schedule when I want -I want to just drive through locations and not stop for 30 min like you want me to. -calendar should be fluid and move as one. Why are you asking for money at this stage? Who is paying you money? You can\'t ask for money for a piece of shit. Great idea! :)

Daniel was both baffled and horrified. What did this rant mean? The poster, whom we'll call Mr. Null, said the app was a piece of you-know-what, but at the same time said it was "the most promising ever." And he ended with a smiley face :).

I told Daniel that within this inarticulate rant there was opportunity.

Opportunity? replied Daniel. For what? A migraine?

I told him that we could learn some important clues from Mr. Null:

▶ Mr. Null wants to engage. He wants to be seen as a "tough guy," but he wants someone to listen to him and engage him. Under the swagger and bluster, deep down inside, he wants to be *liked*.

▶ He never says that he won't use the app. He just says that he won't pay for it. His primary complaint is the cost.

▶ He sees in the app great potential. He wants it to be good. But for some reason, it's not meeting his expectations.

My advice to Daniel was to have his digital communications manager reply to Mr. Null. He or she should say, "Dear Mr. Null: Thanks for your message. We're listening. Here's what we want you to do. List the top three ways we can improve the app. Be specific. And to sweeten the deal, when you reply we're going to give you six months of free service. For the next six months, just drive around town as you always do, and give us weekly reports on how the app is working for you. We want you to be tough on us. Bring it on!"

Every customer complaint is an opportunity. If Mr. Null cooperates, for the cost of six months' service—thirty bucks— Daniel's app company could have a terrific field tester and brand ambassador.

You can bet that the loudmouth Mr. Null will tell everyone in his social circle how amazing the app is!

INSIGHTS: JEFFREY ROHRS, V.P., MARKETING INSIGHTS AT EXACTTARGET, A SALESFORCE.COM COMPANY.

Here are some compelling observations by Jeffrey Rohrs, the dynamic vice president of marketing insights at ExactTarget, a Salesforce.com company. He oversees a team of incredibly passionate folks responsible for ExactTarget's thought leadership, content marketing, and social media efforts. Jeff also produces and co-authors the award-winning *Subscribers, Fans & Followers* Research Series—an ongoing examination of how today's online consumers interact with brands through email, mobile, and social channels. His first book, *Audience: Marketing in the Age of Subscribers, Fans & Followers* (John C. Wiley & Sons Publishing) tackles the flip side of content marketing—proprietary audience development.

As Jeff and I discussed recently, one challenge that does not get enough attention is the three-way relationship of brand, culture, and organization. To implement any sort of marketing technology, you need to answer some basic questions about this relationship. What in the culture of the company is respectful and knowledgeable of the ultimate consumer? Does the brand lend itself to a kind of human, personal voice? And then, ultimately, is the organization structured so it's not siloed for an individual kind of grouplets, and is much more collaborative for achieving company objectives?

Here's an example. Over the last ten years, we've experienced an absolute seismic explosion—a Cambrian explosion—of digital channels. Every year, there's a new digital channel that you have to deal with. An activated marketing organization needs to be very reactionary to that. You've got to put a body on a channel; as a leader you ask, what's our Instagram strategy? What's our Twitter strategy? What's our Pinterest strategy? You may have been very siloed in thinking about them in terms of, "This is an e-mail, this is social, and this is our mobile app." We're now seeing the dust settle on that, where each year brings fewer truly revolutionary channels; they are now much more evolutionary channels. In that context, instead of focusing on a silo channel approach, you can begin to finally look at the ultimate objective. And the ultimate objective is to serve that customer better and, hopefully, increase your share of wallet through positive product and service experience.

If you shift the focus from channel to the outcome, now you're focused on the individual. Now you're focused on important questions like, where does the consumer live? How do they want to operate? How do they want to deal with us? And instead of having wars between channel owners for budget, for emphasis, for priority, we can now have teams that think more holistically about the company's permanent objectives with the consumer. Now the channel has become an execution point instead of the destination.

That's a big challenge for a lot of organizations because they are so hierarchical. A flat organization is not necessarily what is needed to solve this, but an adaptive, collaborative culture certainly is, as well as a brand that has flexibility, humanity, and is willing to experiment.

Jeff is intrigued by these issues and touches upon them in his book. If you read between the lines of different things developing in marketing, you see that success with business technology comes down to a lot of organizational decisions and a lot of the human nature of the organization itself. Absent that passion for the individual and that passion to serve the consumer, you can end up applying the technology in a very dehumanizing way that assumes things that the consumer wants that they really don't.

He wrote an article for Forbes CMO network on the occasion of the fifteenth anniversary of Seth Godin's *Permission Marketing* coming out. If you go back and you read that book, you now realize that permission marketing has taken over the world. That all of these channels we deal with—including, increasingly, visual advertising and the whole EU cookie conversation—are dependent on the consumer giving us permission to market; whereas if you went back twenty years ago, that was never even in question. If you were a direct marketer, you owned a list, and you could mail an advertisement to someone regardless of whether they wanted it or not.

Now, in all of these digital channels, the consumer controls it, and if we ignore permission, and if we ignore their desires, it's at our peril.

FACTS YOU NEED TO KNOW

▶ 70% of companies identify their most important strategic initiative as "improving the brand image through social media."

▶ In a survey where agency respondents chose 3 digital related areas which were their top priorities going forward, the most important categories voted were Multichannel Campaign Management and Content Marketing.

▶ "High quality Twitter followers are 50% more likely to buy products from the brands they follow than their non-follower counterparts."

CHAPTER 4
THE DIGITAL PERSONAL BRAND

Before you have time to think (too much thinking can be hazardous to your health), I want you to take a quick little quiz. It will be fun because there are no right or wrong answers. It will take less than a minute.

The quiz is multiple choice, which makes it even easier. All you have to do is read each statement and choose the best answer of A, B, C, or D.

Ready? OK. Here we go.

1. This person has been extremely successful in business.

A. Hillary Clinton

B. Chris Christie

C. Joe Biden

D. Mitt Romney

2. This person embodies the attitudes and capabilities of Millennials.

A. Derek Jeter

B. Mark Zuckerberg

C. Joe Biden

D. Oprah Winfrey

3. This person is the idol of millions of teenaged girls.

A. Miley Cyrus

B. John McCain

C. Joe Biden

D. Barbara Walters

Okay, I fibbed—there are right and wrong answers. As I'm sure that you'll agree, the best choices are 1 (D), 2 (B), 3 (A).

I included this little quiz to demonstrate the power of personal branding. In each case, it was an easy matter to match up the statement with the best choice. For example, in question 1, regardless of what you may think of Mitt Romney as a candidate for president, and the fact that the other three choices include people who have achieved much, no one can dispute that he best fits the description as someone who has been extremely successful in business.

In the previous chapter I talked about the digital corporate brand, and how it is formed and manipulated by a variety of forces. Individuals have brands, too. In the old days it was called your reputation (as in, "A man's reputation precedes him," or "Don't sully your good reputation.") It tended to have a moral frame; a "bad" reputation was a sign of poor moral character. In contrast, the concept of your personal brand is a bit more nuanced. For example, Miley Cyrus has a very strong personal brand, as do many entertainers. Some people think she's disgraceful. These tend to be people who are not in her market—that is, they wouldn't buy her records no matter what kind of performance she did on television. Her fans—the people who are likely to buy her products—think she's terrific.

In the public arena, personal branding often focuses on self-packaging, where success is determined not by an individual's internal sets of skills, motivations, and experience but by how sharply they are defined. It is more about self-promotion that is deliberately intentional in all aspects because the individual is purposely shaping their image or persona. Personal branding can be used as a marketing and promotional tool to identify an individual as a type of person ("Miley Cyrus is wild and free"). Success on virtual platforms then becomes online social value that can produce real rewards in the offline world.

In a sense, everyone has a personal brand. The kid who wants to date your daughter? "I wouldn't let that slacker within fifty feet of this house!" Your dentist? "Oh, he's wonderful—I never feel a thing!" The woman who lives next door? "She makes the best strawberry preserves!" You get the idea.

Your personal brand may be something that you don't think too much about—that is until it becomes a part of your professional life and your career. Then it can become very important and something that you need to manage and to make an investment in.

You need to activate it.

HOW YOUR PERSONAL BRAND IS CREATED

Much like a corporate brand, in the digital culture your personal brand consists of two sources of information:

▶ Stuff that you create.

▶ Stuff that people say about you, whether you like it or not.

For example, politicians go to extreme lengths to control the information that flows out into the public arena about themselves and their wonderful accomplishments. Unlike most private citizens, politicians must also deal with political opponents who are actively working to flood the digital town square with negative information, whether it's factual or not. Candidates for high office now routinely establish "war rooms" whose sole function is to detect negative information in the public sphere and counterattack with something positive. At the end of the day, the public decides, by voting, whose political brand has managed to stay positive.

A discussion of political branding would easily fill another book, so we'll leave that and turn our focus onto the corporate realm, where the battle may be less intense but where the stakes for your career could be equally high.

Let's talk about the first component of your personal brand—stuff you create.

Facebook, LinkedIn, Twitter, blogs, Skype, texting, YouTube, emails, and other technologies allow us to activate our public personas in ways previously unimaginable. With a mobile device, you can broadcast an event that interests you. You can attract followers on Twitter. You can post your resume on an online job search site for any employer to see. Your vacation photos from Club Med? Let the world see them online. Do you like a particular product? Let your friends know on Pinterest. Got an opinion? Blog about it.

Here's the flip side. The digital town square is a public place. It's full of other people who exchange news and post events. They may even talk about you. This is the stuff that you did not create and may not be able to control.

In the previous chapter, I mentioned attorney Joe Smith, who got himself disbarred for a year. When you Googled his name, the very first result at the top of the page was the screaming headline, "State Supreme Court Suspends Attorney Joe Smith..." While he did not create this story, it was perfectly true. The headline and the story were posted on the official website of the State Supreme Court as a matter of public record. Smith could not have it removed. His only recourse was to create more of his own online brand. He needed positive professional content—on his website, his blogs, Twitter, mentions of him on other websites—to dilute the damage to his brand.

CONFIRMATION BIAS

Just as it can damage you, the stuff that other people say, if properly ignited, can strengthen your brand. In defining her super-activated "wild child" brand, Miley Cyrus has benefitted from thousands of reports, blogs, opinion pieces, and reviews created by third parties who are not on her payroll. By perpetuating and discussing her wild child image, they're unwittingly doing her PR for her. This is an example of a powerful force known as "confirmation bias."

This is simply a syndrome whereby if enough people agree on a certain characteristic of something or someone, when they get new information they will bend it to fit their preconception. Information that contradicts their belief may be rejected.

You learned this in grade school. Remember when you were in class, and one of the kids threw a spitball when the teacher's back was turned? Stung by the nasty projectile, the teacher whirled around … and the kids were all sitting quietly with their hands folded. Yet someone threw the spitball. Was it Johnny, the long-haired kid who always slouched in the back row, or Tony, the clean-cut athlete in the front? Confirmation bias made the teacher accuse Johnny, even though he may have been perfectly innocent.

Take Governor Chris Christie and "Bridgegate." When the story broke about the lane closures on the George Washington Bridge, many people quickly assumed that he had to know about it and that perhaps he had even ordered the lane closures himself to punish a political opponent. Absent any actual evidence, why were people so quick to believe this? Because Chris Christie had built for himself a personal brand of being a tough guy who was not afraid to attack his political opponents. The lane closures were a confirmation of his tough-guy brand, regardless of whether he was personally involved.

MANAGING YOUR DIGITAL PERSONAL BRAND

When people type your name into Google or other search engines, what do they find? Positive information or negative? Information that supports your professional career, or stuff that's silly or irrelevant? Even if you have no digital presence that you have created, there may be stuff online that you don't want and have no power to alter. Therefore, you need to activate your digital brand. You need to take charge and assert the image that you want to project.

Let's go back to Miley Cyrus, who is a terrific case study in corporate branding (yes, Miley is a corporation, with millions in brand income, just like a brand of toothpaste). She began her career in 2006 as an eleven-year-old squeaky-clean teen idol in the Disney Channel television series *Hannah Montana*, in which she portrayed the starring character Miley Stewart. After signing a recording contract with Hollywood Records in 2007, Cyrus released her debut studio album *Meet Miley Cyrus*. She became a wholesome global pop icon of whom parents approved.

But by 2013, she was ready to re-brand herself as an adult star. Miley hired Larry Rudolph, who had previously worked with Britney Spears, to be her new manager. Her 2013 CD Bangerz featured the singles "We Can't Stop" and "Wrecking Ball," and she flooded the airwaves with racy videos and performances that collectively obliterated the Hannah Montana brand image. She's very active in social media. In 2014, she had a reported 18.2 million followers on Twitter. In case you're wondering, in that same year the reigning queen of Twitter was singer Katy Perry, with 53.7 million followers. She was followed by Justin Bieber (52.3 million), President Barack Obama (43.5 million), and You-Tube (42.7 million). Yes, YouTube tweets—about news, music, and trends from its top channels. The top-rated actual human being who is a businessperson was Bill Gates, with 16.2 million followers.

Unless you're happy to live in a cave or on a desert island, you need to invest time and energy into activating your digital personal brand, just like Miley Cyrus, President Obama, and Bill Gates.

By activating your online reputation, and building and promoting your personal brand, you can both dilute the power of unflattering comments and photos, and showcase accomplishments or experiences in the top results when someone searches your name.

✓ **LinkedIn.** For business executives, LinkedIn has become a key site. Make sure that you craft a well-written, professional profile. Be honest, as it's easy to verify or refute the information you provide. Then, you can leverage your account by setting up other accounts in places similar to LinkedIn such as ZoomInfo.com, Workface.com, Naymz.com, Plaxo.com, and BrandYourself.com. Copy your LinkedIn profile and then paste it into these accounts. Adapt the text to fit the site's specific format, and re-write the first few sentences so that the content showing up in a Google search result is different for each site.

✓ **Google+.** Burnish your personal brand by setting up a Google Profile at Google.com/plus. Set up your free account, and then link it to your website and social networks.

✓ **Twitter.** Create an account at Twitter.com and then tweet on a regular schedule. Refrain from tweeting about trivial things like what coffee you bought at Starbucks. Instead, share information that others value, such as articles related to your business or industry. Follow others whose reputations you respect, which in turn could increase your followers.

✓ **Facebook.** Remove any photos that don't show you in a positive professional light. Share information about your personal life, because that's what people want to see on Facebook, but keep it innocuous. Your trip to Mexico? Fine. The subsequent attack of Montezuma's revenge? Skip it—it's TMI. And make sure to set your Facebook Privacy settings to help you control access.

✓ **Be careful when posting or communicating!** The best attitude to have is to believe that every email you send and every online comment that you make can potentially become public. Don't text a friend, send an email, post a tweet, or comment on an online post unless you're sure that what you say is presented in a professional manner that anyone could read.

✓ **Monitor your digital brand**. When was the last time you Googled yourself? (OK—if your answer is, "I Google myself every hour," maybe you need to dial it back a notch.) Negative information spreads like a virus online, and you cannot leave your personal brand and reputation to chance. You can sign up for a free service that will notify you when your name appears online, such as Google Alerts or Topsy.com.

The point is that if even you're only marginally involved in your community or have a modest professional presence, you have a digital brand that may exist without your having created it. It's smart to activate your personal brand: get ahead of the curve and manage what others see about you and say about you online.

FACTS YOU NEED TO KNOW

▶ "72.6% of sales people using social media outperformed sales people who do not use social media."

▶ With the importance of going digital becoming more apparent, the number of marketers who have an app has increased to 47%.

▶ Leaving people to discuss your personal past and brand is rarely good and the less exposure the better

CHAPTER 5
THE INTERSECTION OF CORPORATE AND PERSONAL BRANDS

Chances are if you're like most people in business you either work for or own a company that employs people. Collectively, everyone in the company—from the boardroom to the loading dock—contributes to the public brand of the company. I'm not talking about "brand" in the sense of the graphic logo on the bag of chips. I'm talking about the full array of the company's activities, from its charitable giving (good) to the disastrous oil spill on the coast (very bad). And in today's digital culture, that brand is expressed online in much the same way as your personal brand: by a mix of stuff the company generates, and by the conversation in the digital town square that it cannot control.

Companies that are activated recognize that their employees are human beings who, while at work and at home, are going to be active online. Some of this activity may be directly related to their jobs while some may be purely personal. But it's going to happen, and in fact, it should happen because it can produce positive results that impact the bottom line.

INSIGHTS: GERARD E. SAMPLE, V.P. OF SALES ENABLEMENT, CA TECHNOLOGIES

As Vice President of Sales Enablement at CA Technologies, Gerard E. Sample was globally responsible for providing sellers with the content and methodology essential to articulating value and conducting successful engagements. Specializing in solutions marketing, interactive content development and messaging at the point of sale, Gerard established sales enablement as a newly recognized marketing function at CA Technologies in 2011.

Gerard has contributed in both sales and marketing roles at Internet and technology companies including The Sutherland Group, Match.com, Sun Microsystems, and BlueArc Corporation. As founder of Third Wave Interactive, Gerard Sample now focuses on helping businesses drive new customer acquisition through interactive content.

Gerard believes that the corporate brand is an aggregation of personal brands plus the conscious decision to convey a core message, relevant perspective and market position in an assertive manner. While many people may think, "the brand's just a logo," that lends to any external perception of the organization. This covers a vast amount of ground, starting with what we commonly refer to as standard marketing and PR firm stuff—all culminating in a traditional brand identity package. Here, brand elements such as value proposition, colors, typography, taglines and imagery are typically consistent and centrally managed. However, the means by which your employees engage with customers and online communities through social media is inherently fluid. Every interaction and touch point with a potential prospect, lead, new customer, or long-time account contributes to the credibility or reinforcement of the existing brand, whether in a positive or negative way.

A personal brand is the one thing that must endure regardless of who your employer is. Not only do personal brands contribute to the corporate brand through direct association, but in many respects must supersede and be protected with a level of vigilance by an individual even more aggressively than their stewardship of the corporate brand. This should not be viewed as a trade-off, but rather as a question of where you spend your time. Do you simply re-tweet the company's tweets, or do you spend time establishing your credibility as a thought leader with your own professional capabilities?

Gerard is a huge advocate of measuring the impact of every interaction, and gets very passionate when he sees different parts of an organization creating or communicating inconsistent market facing messages. This practice often backfires and tempers the utopian view of "everything's possible now, we have ubiquitous visibility to every digital touch-point and can proactively manage each customer interaction." Brand identity also quickly breaks down given the number of incremental communication channels that technology enables. Consider that in 2000, when Match.com did an ad campaign, Gerard could calculate return on investment through the number of registrations and ultimate conversions, and then factoring in a new customer's lifetime value and internal rate of return. Simply stated, he could tell you if the campaign worked or not.

Now, because there are so many different channels, all the way down to using the example of an individual re-tweeting a company post, the complexity of creating an accurate picture in aggregate is in many respects much more difficult. The problem is that one bad customer interaction (see the example below of the Worst Tweet Ever) can instantly hurt a brand. The result is increased complexity and risk, and with that comes a requirement to increase your systems and controls not from a draconian perspective but from an enablement perspective.

The sheer volume of information being traded is causing degradation in decisiveness, transparency, and decision-making because now everybody has an opinion. We've all seen the emails that are fifty strings long. And the expectation now is that you respond to an email in fifteen minutes. Many executives spend entire days in meetings or on the phone, not necessarily adding value but rather because everyone's trying to make all information, all decision-making, and all collaboration universally accessible.

A Millennial CEO once said, "I want my employees to text me. That's how I communicate." It's hard to imagine what would happen if ten thousand employees all decided to text the CEO. He wouldn't be able to be effective in his role. We always need to keep in mind the premise that for a given culture, and for a given organization, the leadership has to set the precedent and the example on the most productive and streamlined communication.

Everyone has their personal preference as it relates to picking up the phone versus Skype versus text versus email. The company's culture on how people communicate with one another is predicated by how the executives either request information or engage, both with the folks from the company and externally.

Let's consider the front-line salesperson who interacts with customers and prospects on a regular basis. Upper management cannot, nor should they want to control, what a salesperson says to a customer, emails to them, posts on their Facebook account, and on and on. As a result, it's critical that management help that salesperson understand the new normal of nothing's private, and that everything will and should reflect on the company based on the actions of the individual. As a steward of the brand, you have to know and be cognizant of how your personal brand is impacted by your actions online or even on a one-to-one basis, and how those actions immediately flow up to and either degrade or reinforce the brand promise of the company.

While on the subject of personal interaction, we're seeing too many big enterprises that publish a canned, ghostwritten CEO blog that sounds written by a PR firm. It's not raw, it's not authentic, and it lacks credibility, and what it means is you're not connecting and communicating with your customers in an authentic way that is relevant to them. Many companies are still taking the position of, "We're going to project our brand and not engage in a conversation," whether that's internal or external.

STRIKING THE BALANCE

One key to success as you activate your company is to recognize the balance that the company needs to strike between an employee's legitimate desire and need to build his or her own personal brand, and the need to sublimate the personal brand to that of the company while on the job. By focusing entirely on your personal brand, you reduce your attractiveness as a hire because no company wants a selfish worker who isn't fully dedicated to the goals of the business and who may be suspected of using the business as a personal platform. On the other hand, if you concentrate solely on your company's brand, you may make yourself invisible to your industry.

If you represent your company in the digital town square—even informally—you need to remember that what you say can affect not only you, but your colleagues as well.

INSIGHTS: BRYAN E. JONES, V.P. OF NORTH AMERICA COMMERCIAL MARKETING, DELL

The leader of Dell's North America marketing organization, and Dell's Global 500 accounts, Bryan E. Jones and his team are responsible for marketing end-to-end, spanning all lines of business across Dell for the enterprise, including the company's healthcare and education verticals. His team develops, manages, and executes the marketing strategy in the region, enabling North America sales and serving as a trusted advisor to their customers.

At the 2014 SXSWi conference in Austin, Texas, Bryan spoke at the #DellVenue and MediaPost OMMA conference. In his talk, he reminded his audience that conversations, whether in person or on social media, happen not between computers or disembodied machines but between people. He offered five lessons for empowering employees to participate in the real-time social conversations.

1. Bryan's First Rule of Social Media is simply this: "Don't do dumb things." A company needs to build and support a culture of social, and then let employees run with it. At Dell, the company offers guidelines for their employees through SMAC University. These guidelines include identifying themselves as employees of Dell when they tweet about the company, connecting with customers in meaningful ways. Dell's voice is positive and constructive; team members who engage with customers are reminded that, like the company, their purpose is to be authentic to the Dell brand and to help customers "do more."

2. The volume of social data is less important than the insights and information. The beauty of social engagement is forming an emotional connection with customers; you don't want to squash the life out of it by over-analyzing and applying too many metrics at Dell, the focus is on getting people to let go of big chunks of data, not to get paralyzed by the data. Focus on authenticity and the rest will come naturally.

3. Empower your employees to represent the brand as ambassadors. Putting social in a silo means that only a select few will have conversations with a small number of customers. Abandon the notion of a dedicated team who represents the company in social media, and instead integrate it across the organization. By allowing everyone to participate in the real-time conversation, a company can create a culture of social and make it part of their DNA. Marketing on social is everyone's job, and everyone should have a role.

4. Don't photo-bomb someone else's conversation. Real-time marketing isn't the same thing as news-jacking, a term meaning to jump on trending news by inserting your brand into the conversation. Engage in organic conversations that are meaningful. For example, Dell technology powers different sports teams' IT infrastructure, so the company has a very active and legitimate social engagement on that topic during key moments in time for a particular team. It is relevant to their business and tells a story of their technology.

As an example of news-jacking that backfired, on July 5, 2011 baked goods producer Entenmann's tweeted, "Who's #notguilty about eating all the tasty treats they want?!" This happened to be the same day that accused child murderer Casey Anthony was acquitted in court. The company soon realized its mistake, deleted the tweet, and followed up with the message, "Sorry everyone, we weren't trying to reference the trial in our tweet! We should have checked the trending hashtag first." The company added, "Our #notguilty tweet was insensitive, albeit completely unintentional. We are sincerely sorry."

News-jacking? Don't go there.

5. Let it happen organically. Searching for prime real-time marketing moments can be exhausting and counterproductive. Rather than looking for moments of connection, keep in mind that enhancing customer experience doesn't happen in a straight line or by following a plan. What you can do is to prepare for those authentic moments. Train employees, and arm them with the tools to execute and support their social engagement throughout the year through regular events that reinforce skills on social media and customer engagement best practices.

"The bottom line is that you cannot overthink or over-metric your social media strategy. Being too prescriptive kills the innovation. Give people the right direction, culture, and guidelines, and then leave them room to innovate. You'll be thrilled with what they come up with."

THE WORST. TWEET. EVER.

Here's a good example of why anyone, in their zeal to become activated, should not do dumb things.

In April 2014, US Airways received a tweet from a customer named Elle, who was unhappy that her US Airways flight had sat on the tarmac for an hour, causing her to be late. In the scheme of things, it was a pretty routine communication. The US Airways tweeter replied, "We truly dislike delays too and are very sorry your flight was affected." Still pretty routine. Elle tweeted back, saying that she was unhappy the company had ignored her previous tweets.

Then the US Airways tweeter wrote back, "We welcome feedback, Elle. If your travel is complete, you can detail it here for review and a follow-up: pic.twitter.com/vbeYgCuG25."

The problem was that "pic.twitter.com…" was a link to a flagrantly pornographic photo of a naked woman using a large model jetliner as a sex toy.

About an hour later the offending tweet was pulled down, but it was too late. The digital cat was out of the bag and running around the digital town square.

It turned out that the graphic picture was originally from a German-language amateur porn and shock site. US Airways spokesman Matt Miller told *The New York Daily News* that the tweet "was an honest mistake." On behalf of the airline, Miller said, "first and foremost, we apologize." He also clarified that no employee would be fired over the incident.

The incident seems to have been a comedy of multiple errors. Apparently US Airways was attempting to flag an inappropriate incoming tweet that contained the graphic image. In doing so, the pic.twitter.com URL was copied as well. Then the graphic image was inadvertently pasted into a tweet sent to another user. While the two tweets were live they somehow linked to each other.

What's the bottom line?

I'd say that most observers had a good laugh at the expense of US Airways. No one got hurt, and I'm sure that no member of the flying public abandoned US Airways because of the gaffe. People know that mistakes can happen.

But you can bet that at US Airways and at many other corporations with active Twitter accounts, the word went out: "Don't do dumb things!"

FACTS YOU NEED TO KNOW

▶ In a survey by Alterra Group, 84% of marketers said that Account Based Marketing provided significant benefits to retaining or expanding their customer base.

▶ Branding is so important in the digital age that a company's brand plays a massive role in whether or not an existing customer buys their services or product. In fact, in the majority of companies, existing customers drive over 50% of the revenue.

▶ In today's business culture, "82% of U.S. consumers now research products online before actually buying them." So monitoring your consumer's actions and what they have to say about you is even more important.

CHAPTER 6
GENERATIONAL WARS AND CULTURE GAPS

Here's a familiar little scene that has been repeated over and over again, perhaps even in your own home.

It's morning. A school day. After much cajoling, the sleepy kids are chowing down on their bowls of cereal.

The mother looks sternly at her young son. She says, "You kids have it so easy today. When I was your age, I walked five miles to school!"

Child Number One erupts in gales of laughter. "Gee, Mom, I thought you rode to school in a horse and buggy!"

Child Number Two howls, "Horse and buggy? I thought you rode to school in a chariot!"

Child Number Three chimes in, "Chariot? Mom, I thought you rode to school on the back of a Brontosaurus!"

Mom shakes her head. "You kids will never understand. And put away those cell phones! No texting at the table!"

"C'mon, Mom," says Child Number One. "Everyone does it. Anyway, Judy wants to know what the history assignment was."

"Hey, Mom," says Child Number Two. "The cat just barfed a fur ball onto the floor. I'm gonna post a picture of it on Instagram."

"Don't you dare!" shrieks Mom.

"Oh, look," says Child Number Three as he peers at his phone. "Johnny just got the Yankees logo shaved onto his head!"

"Don't you try that!" says Mom. "No kid of mine will ever become a free advertisement for a baseball team. Let the Yankees pay for their own ads."

Fast-forward ten years. Child Number One—okay, his name is Rick—is sitting in a managers' meeting with his boss. After graduating from college, he's landed a nice job doing marketing for a local office supplies company.

Rick's boss, who is a direct descendant of Emperor Ceo and who's been the marketing director of the company since Frank Sinatra made vinyl records, stands and goes to the easel at the head of the room. He unveils a big graphic mounted on foam core. "Folks," he says, "Take a look at our new magazine ad. We've bought the inside back cover in all the top trade association magazines. Total circulation of this buy is half a million. You can see the response code in the corner of the ad. In the past, we've picked up an average of three new accounts with these magazine ads. We hope to do as well this time."

Rick doesn't know what to say. He doesn't know where to begin. Foam core? Magazine ads? Response codes? Is the boss speaking some sort of foreign language?

His boss looks directly at him. "Rick? Any thoughts?"

"Ummm," says Rick. "Sir, it looks good to me. I mean, for what it is. That is to say, the agency did a nice job. The magazine ad looks good. Do we have any other initiatives? Is this ad part of a larger campaign?"

"A larger campaign?" asks the boss.

"Yes," replies Rick. "You know, maybe with something online?"

Here's where I'll give you, my valued reader, the opportunity to choose your own ending. You have two choices.

A) The boss says, "My young friend, we don't have time for stuff like that. We sell paper and toner to businesses. We don't need to make our lives complicated."

B) The boss replies, "Online? Good idea. Let's get activated! Can you set up a Facebook page? Can you figure out some metrics for measuring our online conversion rates from our website? How about a live chat feature? Let's talk about it!"

In the 1960s, this difference between Rick and his boss was dubbed the "Generation Gap." In the arc of human history, it's a relatively new phenomenon. It happens when someone who enters the world twenty-five years after his or her parents experiences a culture that is very different from the one his or her parents lived through. The world of the old folks seems distant and incomprehensible.

It wasn't always this way. Think about a kid born in England in the year 1550 (to choose a random year). Let's say his parents were born in 1525. Do you think that anything changed between 1525 and 1550, especially in a rural area? The family lived in the same house, worked the same fields, read the same family Bible, and wore the same clothes as their parents and grandparents. There was no Generation Gap.

Now think about a kid born in 1990. By 2014, he or she would be ready to enter the workforce. He'd be armed with a viewpoint and set of beliefs that he formed as the result of his upbringing. Meanwhile, his or her parents were probably born in 1965. The world was vastly different, and so were their experiences. Mom and Dad grew up with no digital culture—no home or office computers, no Internet and no smartphones. In school, they performed computations on slide rules. The household mechanical dial phone was hard-wired to the wall. A film was something that existed only on a long piece of tape.

Why is this divide important? Precisely for the reason described in the scenario with Rick and his boss. It's important because of what needs to happen in a company both *internally* and *externally*.

THE INTERNAL DIVIDES

If you visit a typical company that has more than a few employees, you'll see people of different ages working together. The boss may be sixty years old. The managers might be forty. The junior staff might be in their twenties. Mixed in here and there might be some older folks who are "lifers"—the ones who are content to remain at mid-level posts for decades.

It's an axiom of business that for an enterprise to thrive, you need to build a team that works harmoniously together. You need internal transparency, a common set of beliefs, and shared viewpoints. The corporate world is replete with examples of companies that broke apart because of conflicts within the corporate culture. Perhaps one of the most oft-cited cases is the 1998 merger of Chrysler and Daimler-Benz. Highly touted as a groundbreaking deal, by 2007 the Frankenstein monster was put out of its misery with Chrysler's sale to Cerberus Capital.

"We obviously overestimated the potential of synergies," Dieter Zetsche, chief executive of what was then called DaimlerChrysler, said at a news conference at the company's headquarters in Stuttgart, Germany. "I don't know if any amount of due diligence could have given us a better estimation in that regard."

Analysts were quick to point out what seemed obvious. Firstly, the management attitude was quite different. Daimler was a very hierarchical company with a clear chain of command and respect for authority. Chrysler, on the other hand, favored a more team-oriented and egalitarian approach. Daimler valued product reliability and achieved the highest levels of quality while Chrysler was known for flashy designs at competitive prices. These two factors created conflicting orders and goals in different departments. American and German managers had different values, and different departments pulled in opposing directions.

When focusing on digital culture, the gap is likely to be less cultural and more generational. It can nonetheless be crippling. Younger employees—as I'll discuss in more depth—may have a point of view that's very different from their colleagues who are even just a decade older.

EXTERNAL ALIGNMENT

Just as management and employees of a company need to form a cohesive team internally, it's just as important to align the company with its external marketplace. Much has been made over the years of the necessity of "relating" to young buyers, because most brands want to become accepted by younger consumers who will then remain loyal for years to come. In the young adult clothing industry, for example, this is particularly acute, and it's been a traditional practice for companies to send out scouts to literally walk the streets and see what kids are wearing. The guy who owns the clothing company may be sixty years old, but if he's smart, he'll listen to his college-aged scouts who may today be surfing Facebook and Pinterest. While he may not have a deep personal understanding of digital culture, he's savvy enough to know that his company needs to get activated, and he'll hire the right people to do it.

FROM THE GREATEST GENERATION TO GENERATION X

In sorting out the various viewpoints held by different age groups, most observers have come to agree on a set of definitions that allow us to talk about age groups and their general characteristics. You've probably heard the terms, but just to keep everyone up to speed, here's a quick recap.

THE GREATEST GENERATION

Also called Matures and the Silent Generation. This roughly encompasses people who directly experienced the four years of World War Two, which for most Americans was a profound transition into the modern era. The Silent Generation, also known as the "Lucky Few," is a subset of those who were born from 1925 until 1942, and includes most of those who fought the Korean War and many during the Vietnam War.

Born before 1945, during the post-war era of the 1950s most Matures were both happy and very grateful to have life return to "normal" and to enjoy the benefits of the rapidly expanding consumer culture. This experience helped define them as loyal, patriotic, and socially conservative.

Interestingly, people in this group have become major users of social media sites like Facebook. This fact highlights an important message of this book: that to be activated and to leverage every aspect of digital culture means going far beyond using social media. Just because Grandma is an enthusiastic user of Facebook does not mean she's fully activated!

BABY BOOMERS

Born between 1946 and 1964, the Boomers experienced the nineteen-fifties post-war era as a time of unprecedented growth and prosperity. A middle-class couple could own a home and a car, and the husband could expect to work for a big corporation for the duration of his career. Baby Boomers were the first generation to be marketed to specifically as children, and the explosion of television made national branding possible on a mass scale. Boomers also witnessed significant social upheavals—political assassinations, riots and protests, the Civil Rights movement, Women's Liberation and the Pill.

After the assassination of President Kennedy and the ugliness of Vietnam began to be pumped into every living room, the huge Boomer segment—one of the biggest population bubbles in history—consciously rejected many of the cherished values of the previous Mature generation. Boomers tended to think of themselves as a special generation, different from those who had come before them. In the 1960s, as the large numbers of young people became teenagers and young adults, around their cohorts they created a very specific rhetoric of music, literature, and film. Remember, though, that the Boomers grew up in an analog, non-digital universe and to become fully activated generally requires training.

GEN XERS

Born between 1965 and 1977, it's a smaller group than the Baby Boomers. Author Douglas Coupland popularized the term "Generation X" in his 1991 book *Generation X: Tales for an Accelerated Culture,* and the name stuck. Gen Xers came of age during a time of cultural drift marked by the post-Watergate national malaise, rising divorce rates, the Iran hostage crisis, the Challenger disaster, Wall Street scandals, and the first cases of AIDS. This group rode the waves of the corporate greed of the 1980s, and they experienced the first tremors of the digital revolution as information became both powerful and suddenly very cheap.

MILLENNIALS

They were born between 1978 and 1995, as a new millennium was dawning. Their early lives were marked by 9/11 and the Oklahoma City bombing, the Columbine shooting, and the Iraq War. But this is the first generation for whom digital communication is ubiquitous. There's an adage for middle-aged Boomers that goes, "If you don't know how to fix your computer, just ask any Millennial. The kid will reboot it in no time." Millennials take instant global communication for granted and regard traditional interruption marketing—things like TV commercials—as disposable. For Millenials, it's both easier and more logical to get product information from their peers than from product manufacturers.

GENERATION Z

This is a name used by some for the cohort of people born after the Millennial Generation. There is no agreement on the exact dates of the generation, with some sources starting it at the mid- or late-1990s or from the mid-2000s. This is the generation that is currently being born, and for whom things like same-sex marriage, non-white-male US presidents, and legalized marijuana will presumably be just a normal part of life.

In your workplace, these are the folks who can make life miserable for each other if they're not brought together, and who can also work wonders by sharing their experiences and talents towards one common goal. When you set the goal to activate your organization and leverage the power of the digital toolbox, one of the first tasks that you need to tackle is to make sure that every member of your team is personally activated and understands their role in an activated company.

FACTS YOU NEED TO KNOW

▶   In a study by Pew Research Center, it was found that 95% of Millennials own a cell phone while only 84% of Baby Boomers own a cell phone.

▶   Change needs to come, and come fast as "By 2017, Millennials will have more spending power than any other Generation in America."

▶   39% of Millennials surveyed write about their negative experiences with products or companies online.

CHAPTER 7
IT'S THE PEOPLE, STUPID!

Given the often profound differences in cultural orientation that we see between the Greatest Generation, Boomers, GenX, and Millennials, what's the solution for creating an activated, transparent organization that's fully engaged with both its own employees and the marketplace?

Here's a hint: The answer is not in just buying a bunch of hardware and software. It's in creating a human-centered culture of innovation, transparency, and agility that's fully engaged with our increasingly digital culture.

What I call "digital-itis" is a serious disease. But the "digital" part of it is simply a reflection of current trends in technology.

This isn't the first time that human beings have been to this rodeo. To illustrate, let's go back to the year 1455 when Johannes Gutenberg, a metal worker, invented the first functional printing press featuring moveable type. With this amazing innovation, a full page of written materials could be quickly assembled and printed at one time. Gutenberg's first mechanically printed publication was the Bible, subsequently known as the Gutenberg Bible.

The Catholic Church fiercely resisted the printing press. For over a thousand years, the scriptures had been held, copied, and interpreted by priests. The Church feared that if it could not limit access to the scriptures, including its own interpretations of them, it would lose control over its followers.

Thanks to the printing press, the Bible became widely available. For the first time, large numbers of lay people were able to read and see the text for themselves. The popularized Bible served, above all, the interests of the new bourgeoisie. Ancient boundaries and divisions—the old feudal system that preserved differences of caste, divided the masses, and cemented the rule of powerful regional monarchs—had hindered the emerging merchant class. New interpretations of the Bible became an important instrument for breaking the monopoly of the Church and monarchies, and enabling the merchant class to push society in the direction of powerful nation-states as opposed to dozens of regional fiefdoms.

It had long been a crime to even translate the Bible, much less print one outside of the control of the Church. In 1521, William Tyndale, an Oxford scholar living in Antwerp, began to translate the Latin Bible into English. He did so because he was distressed that the people of England were scripturally illiterate. Tyndale translated the Bible into English, printed copies of his version at Antwerp, and illegally smuggled the Bibles into England. In 1535, he was betrayed by a fellow Englishman, convicted of heresy, and burned at the stake. His last words, reportedly, were, "Lord, open the king of England's eyes!"

With every advance in technology comes resistance. This underscores the idea that technology alone is not sufficient to bring progress; it must be tested, evaluated, embraced, and made a part of the fabric of the culture.

Luckily, no one at your company is going to get burned at the stake for becoming a champion of digital culture. But as you make the move to activate your organization, something more insidious may happen: opposition by what I call the anti-digital dinosaurs.

ANTI-DIGITAL DINOSAURS

For those who were not born into a digital culture, embracing digital change can be hard. To make it work in your company, you first need the buy-in of people who will adapt your processes and embrace the potential unleashed when you activate.

We've all been in those executive management meetings when hard decisions about marketing and big data had to be made. Should we cut the program? Should we change our content marketing strategy? Marketing decisions can be hard to make if objective data is scarce, and, typically, there are more opinions than individuals in any given meeting.

What irritates me to no end is when the strategic marketing decision meeting becomes a game of "Dinosaurs in the Boardroom." Haven't heard of it? Oh yes, there is an app for that, and it's called "Corporate Politics 101." If you stand a chance of fully activating your next campaign, you might just want to use the cheat sheet below as a way of quickly identifying the corporate anti-digital-change dinosaurs who will try to prevent you from soliciting real meaningful insights and feedback.

✓ The Corporate Naysayer. Despite an abundance of empirical data, the corporate naysayer dinosaur refuses to acknowledge any form of accountability for inferior client satisfaction, low ratings, or honest feedback received from marketing research. They often use phrases like, "That's news to me," or, "Can we verify that?" as if they never took the time to probe the pulse of an irate client to understand the root cause of their problem.

✓ The Corporate Head-Nodder. He's smart enough to pretend that he's listening and processing your data, and might even ask a few questions to build rapport along the lines of, "Interesting statistic, what does it mean?" He makes it appear that he speaks no evil and might support your digital change plan. But behind the smiling face, he's just toying with you. He has no intention of supporting change because it means he'll have to work slightly harder.

✓ The Corporate Stick-in-the-Mud. Equipped with a unique DNA strand of the ability to think only about their own cubicle and not to see beyond their own silo, the corporate non-visionary comments on your digital marketing change only through the narrow perspective of what they see an inch from their nose. They often use phrases like, "I don't think this would work for my department" or, "Well, mobile apps are not secure," and sometimes will even say, "Our clients aren't online" despite clear evidence that the competition is online, activated, and ready for a higher level of engagement.

Surrounded by these corporate dinosaurs, what should an evolved marketer do? Here are three quick tips.

1. Murder-board it. Using a media training technique borrowed from the Pentagon that prepares military officers for external media scrutiny by rehearsing the worst case scenarios, the tough questions and objections that should be addressed before you make your presentation. Playing devil's advocate ensures that your genuine desire for change doesn't get killed by one of the above-noted dinosaurs.

2. Role play and simulate the three dinosaurs. Simulate and anticipate their answers, given your unique company culture and internal politics. Is there a point of getting the buy-in prior to the meeting to ensure that you get a dinosaur to wake up and smell the coffee?

3. Map out three positive choices. If you're going into a meeting expecting the dinosaurs to give you a clear "yes" or

"no" on one proposal, you should be prepared for a "no," because most people are looking for ways to avoid risk. However, if you build three realistic scenarios where you are giving them a "yes," another "yes," or a third "yes" with different configurations, you may get what you want out of the same ineffective crew.

Bottom line: Call it "change management," "surviving the jungle," or "survival of the fittest," be cognizant of the three corporate dinosaurs who are blocking your company from becoming digitally savvy. If you're not, you may wind up going extinct just like them.

INSIGHTS: MARK STOUSE, V.P. OF GLOBAL CONNECT AT BMC SOFTWARE

As the vice president of global connect at BMC Software, a $2.2 billion enterprise software company, Mark Stouse leads, designs and operationalizes powerful programs that influence multiple audiences and interest groups. He created and implemented the communications strategy regarding a major activist shareholder, culminating in the privatization of BMC in 2013. He continued to pioneer and innovate the "investment fund" approach represented by the ISS platform, combining predictive analytics and proven, contemporary approaches to magnetize the company and drive gains in demand generation, deal expansion and sales velocity. He returned to BMC Software from Honeywell Aerospace, where he was leading a global marketing and communications team.

Mark says that to activate is not merely a function of the platform choice but a function of change management and culture. Particularly in this day and age where there are so many people active in social channels, if you have a situation where— let's say—you introduce Chatter into your company and you've really promoted it, socialized it, and had little tutorials, and you still have very low adoption, that's a cultural problem. It's probably because people are afraid to use it.

In a company he once worked for, that was exactly the case. He had to go to the leadership of the company with a lot of data and say, "Look, fair or unfair, right or wrong, people are afraid to use this. So we now need to decide what we think about this and if we care about this. Almost sociologically speaking, we need to be thankful that this platform introduction has actually revealed this cultural bias to us, so that we can resolve it. Then adoption of the platform will become a metric of successful change management in the culture."

If you're not willing to have those kinds of tough conversations, you're never going to have a seat at the table. There are a lot of reasons why people get seats at tables, but being willing to step up and have the hard conversation in an acceptable, self-aware and effective way, is part of it.

There needs to be a lot of courage in the boardroom and courage by key management, no matter which area of communications in the company, to actually align the needs with the wants and have a deep understanding of what it means to activate. Without it, any effort becomes burdensome technology: an unmitigated disaster one way or the other.

THE COST OF THE FAILURE TO ACTIVATE

Allowing the dinosaurs to block progress can be costly. To better understand how businesses succeed or fail to use digital technology to improve business performance, in 2013 MIT Sloan Management Review and Capgemini Consulting conducted a survey that garnered responses from 1,559 executives and managers in a wide range of industries. The survey and subsequent report focused on digital transformation, which was defined as the use of new digital technologies (social media, mobile, analytics, or embedded devices) to enable major business improvements such as enhancing customer experience, streamlining operations or creating new business models. In short, to activate.

The survey responses revealed that while many managers are confident in the ability of technology to bring transformative change to business, many say that their leaders lack the sense of urgency, and fail to embrace a vision for how technology can transform the business. Those companies that successfully activate tend to have leaders who share their vision and define a road map, create cross-organizational authority for adoption, and reward employees for working towards it.

The key findings from the MIT/Capgemini survey are:

▶ According to 78% of respondents, achieving digital transformation will become critical to their organizations within the next two years.

▶ However, 63% said the pace of technology change in their organization is too slow. The most frequently cited obstacle to digital transformation was "lack of urgency."

▶ Only 38% of respondents said that the digital transformation was a permanent fixture on their CEO's agenda.

▶ Where CEOs have shared their vision for digital transformation, 93% of employees feel that it is the right thing for the organization.

The world is going through a digital transformation as everything—customers and equipment alike—becomes connected. The connected world creates a digital imperative for companies. They must succeed in creating transformation through technology, or they'll face being overtaken by competitors that do.

Even in a connected world, it takes time, effort, and stamina to achieve significantly transformative effects from new technology. Employees know that technology matters: a solid majority of respondents said achieving digital transformation will become critical to their organizations within the next two years. 81% said their organizations were already trying to achieve digital transformation. Less than five percent of respondents say digital transformation will never become important for their organizations.

"The big thing is, technology change is happening so rapidly that every industry is being affected by this," said George Westerman, the research scientist at MIT's Center for Digital Business, and one of the investigators leading the Center's Digital Transformation Research.

Previous research by Capgemini Consulting and MIT's Center for Digital Business found that companies that invest in important new technologies and manage them well are more profitable than their industry peers. Respondents to the survey overwhelmingly believe that failure to effectively conduct digital transformation will harm their company's ability to compete.

FACTS YOU NEED TO KNOW

▶ According to ExactTarget, 80% of marketers say that mobile already does or in the future will provide Return on Investment.

▶ Worldwide mobile transactions will hit up to one-trillion dollars by 2015.

CHAPTER 8
THE ROLE OF MARKETING AUTOMATION

When many managers of the non-digital persuasion—the descendants of Emperor Ceo, who are in the dark either by deliberate choice or simply because they haven't yet been exposed to digital media—envision "digital culture," they often instinctively think of a bunch of kids tapping away on Twitter or posting photos of their drunk frat-party friends on Facebook. And while social media is a big part of the picture, there's much more that takes place behind the scenes, out of sight of the consumer.

In the fully activated organization, the digital revolution has penetrated right down to the trenches of customer identification, acquisition, sales, and retention.

Think about it this way. Any company's marketing efforts can take one of two directions:

▶ You open the door to your store, and serve whoever happens to walk in. There are many businesses that follow this approach. Few of them are either long-lived or profitable.

▶ You make an effort to attract prospects, nurture their interest, learn about what they need, sell them what they want, and follow up to see how they're doing. This approach, which is a proven road to success, takes three things: effort, information, and the right tools.

In the old days, approach #2 was accomplished with old-school tools like index card files, junk mail lists, magazine ads, customer complaint phone numbers, and telemarketer cold-calling. Today, while some of these methods have their place, the process of information collection and interpretation has been made much more powerful by digital technology.

"Marketing automation" is a key component of the move to activate. It broadly refers to software platforms and technologies designed for organizations and their marketing departments to both automate repetitive tasks and to engage their markets on multiple digital channels including email, social media, and websites. Marketing professionals are able to specify criteria and outcomes for goals and processes. These are then interpreted, stored, and executed by software, increasing efficiency and reducing human error. The advantage of a marketing automation platform is that it can streamline sales and marketing processes by replacing high-touch and repetitive manual tasks, such as data entry and statistical analysis, with automated solutions.

Originally focused on email marketing strategies, marketing automation has developed to include a broad range of automation and analytic tools for marketing, especially inbound marketing, which is when you target a core audience by providing useful and quality content to entice them into finding out more about your products or services. You basically give them something in order to get them to come to you.

The basis of marketing automation is software, of which there are three categories.

Marketing automation platforms focus on moving sales leads from where they first enter at the top of the marketing funnel through to becoming sales-ready leads at the bottom of the funnel. It's a push-pull process. Based on their activities, prospects are categorized and then engaged with drip campaign messaging via email and social channels, thus nurturing them from first interest through to sale. Commonly used in business-to-business (B2B), or longer sales cycle business-to-consumer (B2C) sales cycles, marketing automation is a combination of email marketing technology and a traditional sales process that involves coordinated facets of marketing.

Marketing intelligence uses tracking codes in social media, email, and webpages to follow the behavior of anyone who has shown an interest in a product or service. The goal is to assess a level of intent. It can record which social media group or conversation thread the prospect followed, if an email was opened and a link was clicked, or which search term was used to locate a website. Multiple link analysis is able to track buyer behavior; following links and multiple threads related to a product will reveal an interest in that product. This allows for a precisely formulated response and the development of a nurturing program specifically targeted towards the interest of the prospect.

Due to its interactive nature, this has often been dubbed Marketing Automation 2.0.

Advanced workflow automation includes automation of internal marketing processes. These include the marketing calendar, budgeting and planning, workflow and approvals, internal collaboration, digital asset creation, and management—essentially everything that supports the operational goals of the internal marketing function. Typically, these systems require a qualified administrator to set up a clearly defined series of rules to trigger action items for internal sales and marketing staff to process. This type of system increases the marketer's ability to deliver relevant content to selected individuals at appropriate times.

SMART AUTOMATION

A key concept that the dinosaurs in your company might want to know and appreciate is that unlike automated *manufacturing* processes, automated marketing systems aren't designed to replace human beings. Their goal is to make you more effective and make your work more productive. They will give you more time while not compromising the authenticity of the content you're producing. And they will help you reach your goals more quickly.

I mentioned before that marketing automation—or indeed digital marketing in general—is not just about the technology. For example, thousands of ill-informed marketers rely on blanket email marketing to generate leads. They send an email blast after email blast to their massive list of prospects and customers, hoping to get the coveted two-percent response rate, and from that a handful of new customers. But does it work? Not very well.

Sending out email blasts is no different than putting junk mail in someone's mailbox. You're wasting your valuable time and money marketing to someone who may not be interested in what you've got to sell. Even worse, you could be burning your list—that is, annoying your contacts and causing them to mark you as spam, leaving you with no opportunity to market to them in the future.

When well managed, marketing automation allows you to nurture your leads through the entire buying process, delivering highly targeted, personalized messages that address their specific barriers to purchase.

As an example, here's what a simple automated email work-flow might look like:

1. To a targeted list of contacts, you send an email invitation to download your latest ebook. The key is that you *offer* your recipient something useful.

2. Let's say that out of ten thousand people to whom you sent the email, after a period of a day, one thousand had downloaded the ebook. You send a thank-you email to these people.

3. A week later, you send a follow-up email to the list of people who downloaded the ebook, offering them an additional case study relating to that topic.

4. Let's say that one hundred people download the case study. These prospects are showing great interest. Your sales team should get a notification so they can follow up with them.

To manage this kind of simple campaign without marketing automation software would be extremely labor intensive. Now multiply this by a hundred, and add in social media and other digital arenas that automation can leverage, and you can see how productivity can skyrocket.

The ultimate goal of your marketing effort is to generate more revenue for your company. To accomplish this, you need to drive traffic to your website, convert that traffic into leads, and close those leads into customers. Where marketing automation really makes an impact are in the conversion and closure stages of this process.

INSIGHTS: GINA CASAGRANDE, CONTENT EVANGELIST AT ADOBE

Gina Casagrande is a Personalization Evangelist and Team Lead at Adobe with over 15 years of digital marketing experience. An expert in A/B/N and multivariate testing, as well as behavioral targeting optimizations, she is focused on helping customers understand how they can use analytics-based decision-making to deliver exceptional and targeted customer interactions across online marketing channels including search, display, email, social, mobile and website, leading to increased conversions and customer loyalty. Casagrande works with Adobe's largest and most strategic accounts to realign their business strategies, build out their optimization programs, use targeting to drive their personalization efforts, and pivot their marketing directives to become more customer-centric and improve their ROI. As a professional spokesperson for Adobe, she presents Adobe's strategy, roadmap and vision at industry events and conferences globally.

To any organization that needs to step up its marketing automation, Gina offers time-tested advice.

Measurement of ROI is always an area of intense interest. Gina says that it's important to have a solid analytics baseline to understand where you can move the needle and increase your ROI in your marketing efforts. The key to her customers' success begins with setting strategic objectives tied to testing and optimization, executing, and then evangelizing that ROI across the organization. They realize that testing and optimization is like a gym membership—it's a habit that must be consciously developed to succeed. The more you go to the gym, the more you get out of it, and if you don't go at all, it's unlikely you'll reap the rewards. Adobe's customers are using real-time data to analyze results as they come in to quickly refine, and further optimize, their campaigns.

For example, one of her customers, a leading, worldwide PC manufacturer, saw impressive gains in click-throughs and revenue per customer by simply revising the placement of the company's PC finder tool and making a free shipping message more prominent in the site. The ROI learned from their testing and optimization activities, and the fact that they evangelized those results internally, led them to significantly increase their optimization team headcount, and to scale their testing program and resources globally.

Leveraging digital technology has to be done strategically. The most pervasive hurdle is that prospects and customers interact with a brand in not just one way, but in any number of ways including email, mobile site, and comments on a Facebook page. You need to find a way to unify all of that diverse data and all of those interaction points to fully know the whole person and deliver a personalized experience for him or her.

Adobe works to close that gap by providing a single, comprehensive view of a customer—a master marketing profile across all of its digital solutions. Marketers are delivered actionable insights in real time, enabling them to measure, personalize, and optimize their campaigns and digital experiences instantly and across channels.

In terms of technology trends, the personal health and wellness software and services industry is expected to increase dramatically thanks in large part to the wearable tech market. There will be a great opportunity for marketers to introduce a new generation of deeply interactive marketing through wearables.

Consumers today expect brands to deliver relevant, personalized experiences across websites, mobile, and other online channels. The challenge for marketers over the next few years is to deliver those personalized experiences to millions of distinct and demanding customers. Scaling those efforts will be difficult, so automated personalization—targeting informed by self-learning algorithms that determine and serve relevant content—will be key to marketers' future efforts.

Gina is increasingly seeing organizations juggling a higher volume of rich media assets such as photography, banners, and video across a variety of channels like web, mobile, and social sites. More companies are expected to employ dynamic content that can deliver these types of media in real-time across all digital channels, with efficiency and scale.

As for mobile, Gina is increasingly seeing consumers shop socially, search locally, and do this all on mobile devices. That means that we'll continue to see innovations like geofencing, which provides companies the opportunity to create, manage, and deliver highly personalized mobile app experiences in real-time based on location. In addition, bricks-and-mortar companies will begin to leverage iBeacon technology to bridge the gap between digital and in-store experiences to deliver more targeted content to their visitors.

And perhaps even further down the line, Gina expects that we'll be seeing innovations that leverage the best of the digital and analog worlds. In 2013 Adobe introduced an exploration called Project Context that infuses how magazine layouts are created today—in some cases physically with paper, scissors, and boards—with an operating system-like experience featuring multiple connected screens, as well as touch and gesture interaction.

The potential for marketing automation is vast. According to Jupiter Research, conversion rates can soar up to 400 percent higher for targeted campaigns versus campaigns that don't use targeting. It's not surprising that some experts predict that the marketing automation industry will grow to $4.8 billion by 2015.

Marketing automation should allow marketers to determine which visitor groups or segments receive content that's relevant to them, as well as provide actionable insights that they can then respond to. As long as there's a system that combines automation with human controls, so they can ensure it meets their business objectives, there's no downside to marketing automation.

FACTS YOU NEED TO KNOW

▸ **"Marketing automation drives a 14.5% increase in sales productivity and a 12.2% decrease in marketing overhead."**

▸ **The Cisco Visual Networking Index says that in 2014, mobile data traffic has experienced 81% growth in just a year.**

▸ **"25% of all Fortune 500 companies and 76% of the largest SaaS providers are using marketing automation."**

CHAPTER 9
ACTIVATE YOUR MARKETING AUTOMATION

When used correctly, marketing automation can be a powerful tool. It helps large companies to connect with each of their customers in a personalized way that would otherwise be highly labor intensive. It allows small businesses with limited staff resources to run complex campaigns successfully and to leverage their time more efficiently.

Getting activated with an automated marketing solution can be transformative for your business, whether large or small. Here are the top ten benefits of marketing automation solutions.

▸ **Leverage staff resources.** With automated solutions, a single staff member can execute multiple, ongoing campaigns, and can forge a connection with many more customers than would be possible manually.

▸ **Save time.** Staff can create multiple campaigns and posts ahead of time and schedule them to be released at a specific time and date. A marketing manager could, for example, create an entire month's worth of blog posts in one day and set them to post throughout the month.

▸ **Save money.** For a small business looking to efficiently manage their budget, marketing automation can provide low-cost solutions. Time is money, and by reducing the time and effort spent by staff creating and distributing messages and collecting data, a company can make the most of its human capital.

▶ **Target unique customers.** Instead of manually segmenting customers based on their needs and preferences, specialized marketing automation solutions allow a manager to specify restrictions that will allow customers to be automatically sorted. For example, an electronics supply company could instruct the solution to create a list of builders who have purchased HVAC control systems for office buildings. The solution can then send messages and promotions to those customers that relate specifically to that application. This way, customers receive messages that are relevant to their individual needs.

▶ **Communicate consistently.** Manually posting to Twitter or Facebook is inherently undependable and the frequency will be impacted by work and other distractions. If posts or tweets are automated and scheduled, the account stays current so visitors know that you are an active and engaged business. An inconsistently updated social media account won't develop the necessary follower loyalty that is needed to maintain a close connection with the market.

▶ **Keep workflow simple**. Even for people who are not technically adept, marketing automation can be easy to manage. With most automated marketing solutions that are now available, staff do not need specialized design or coding experience to create effective campaigns. Many solutions offer ubiquitous templates, easy-to-use editors, and clear directions to guide staff through the process of creation and distribution.

▸ **Get detailed reports.** Automated marketing solutions can track each email campaign, text message, and Facebook post. Detailed graphs, statistics, and other report data can be generated, providing the ability to evaluate current campaigns and optimize future campaigns. Having data from all campaigns automatically collected and organized makes it simple to produce actionable reports.

▸ **Maintain brand consistency.** Maintaining a consistent brand helps customers to identify your business and connect with the company. Marketing automation makes it possible for any business to present a consistent brand presence on multiple channels. Some automated marketing solutions offer multiple channels in a single solution. Based on a uniform brand message, campaigns can be expanded across multiple channels such as email, YouTube, Facebook, Twitter, text messages, and more. Encouraging customers to interact with the business through multiple channels makes it easy for customers to connect in a way that is convenient for them, and it increases the brand's visibility and helps attract new customers.

▸ **Build customer profiles.** Marketing automation helps a company gather information based on customers' purchases, preferences, email opens and responses, and more. The data can be stored for future use, to allow automated campaigns to be quickly created to reach out to each customer more effectively.

▸ **Nurture leads more effectively.** Connecting with each lead manually can be very time-consuming. With an automated marketing solution, a company can reach out to a potential lead from the very beginning of the interaction. For example, if a customer visits the company website and downloads a free ebook, the manager can connect with them right away with an automated solution. The prospect can receive a welcome message, confirmation, and even a discount coupon and survey about their preferences.

KNOW YOUR VISITOR

Remember Emperor Ceo? As he was being fleeced by Slick & Shark, there were people in the kingdom who tried to voice their opinions about the dire state of the kingdom's clothing industry. But many of these people—subjects who were fearful of the emperor, or just ordinary citizens who weren't ready to sign their names at the bottom of a piece of parchment—remained anonymous. Even if Emperor Ceo heard their comments, what could he do? Take action based on vague and untagged Internet chatter?

An activated enterprise thrives on market knowledge that is both collected in real time and detailed enough to support a targeted response. Imagine if Emperor Ceo had access to today's ubiquitous real-time marketing intelligence tools that could help him make actionable decisions about key projects and products. By getting activated, he could have saved himself and his kingdom the embarrassment and cost of the disastrous Slick & Shark wardrobe rollout.

If your business's marketing department isn't able to currently tell in real time who is visiting your website, what their purchase intent is, and provide caller ID-like intelligence to business development, you might as well declare yourself a relic of the middle ages and use parchment for your marketing reports.

Right now, as you're reading this book, activated corporate marketers are embedding marketing intelligence technology services that allow them to link a digital visitor to any corporate communication objective including branding, public relations, reputation management, sales, and business development. And all of this information is sent via email straight to their inbox in real time.

These savvy marketers can even design and profile (score) each digital corporate visitor and customize the reporting so that your C-suite (command control) is informed of any and all new potential business leads.

Some readers might say, "Gee, isn't it creepy to collect this information before a sales prospect has actually called or filled out a form on my site?" No, it's not. Implemented correctly and acted upon ethically, "know your visitor" (KYV) is not just a pre-sales intelligence tool but a powerful strategic communications overlay that can help your entire brand communications operations succeed and remain in-the-know.

Some real business application scenarios that we advise B2B clients to engage this technology include:

▶ **Real-time competitive marketing intelligence.** Let's say that a big RFP is out, and your business development team is trying to figure out what the competition is doing and who is checking you out. With visitor intelligence software, you can send that intelligence in seconds to your BD capture team and allow them to adjust their strategic messaging for the "win theme" accordingly.

▶ **Real-time crisis communications.** Wouldn't you like to know if a reporter visited your website before they ambushed your CEO to dig up dirt? In fact, wouldn't you like to know what media groups are repeatedly snooping around your corporate site? (By the time Emperor Ceo found out about adverse coverage of the wardrobe rollout, it was much too late!)

▶ **Real-time recruitment communications.** When you're seeking candidates with certain demographics—for instance, if you're looking to hire someone who is currently working for one of your competitors—a huge lead for your human capital chief lies in knowing which companies have been visiting your career page repeatedly. Conversely, you can use this information to form a preemptive strike to keep the competition from poaching your talented team.

▶ **Real-time business impact and metrics for communications campaigns.** With visitor intelligence at your fingertips, you don't have to wait until a campaign is over to see which content marketing campaigns drove traffic and created buzz—and which ones didn't. That's like Emperor Ceo finally taking a look at himself in the mirror after the big parade! It's too late—the damage has already been done. Campaign performance can be analyzed in real-time and reported to your C-suite to maintain corporate buy-in, proving the real value of activated marketing intelligence.

You might be wondering which are the best visitor intelligence technologies available. Many of the leading providers are using publicly available data links that interface with their software. With these types of mixed-source software platforms, a visitor logging in from a corporate domain that has a profile on LinkedIn and/or has been captured by Dun & Bradstreet or Data.com is highly likely to come with a high level of detailed information, down to accurate email addresses of the top decision makers at the visitor's company. Six solid options to consider include CallidusCloud, Marketo, Pardot, NetSuite CRM+, Eloqua, and SalesForce.com.

GETTING ACTIVATED

So how do you become a cutting-edge analyst for your marketing organization and reap these incredible business benefits?

Step 1 – Select a marketing communications agency that can help identify and prioritize the critical marketing intelligence data points that provide instant value to your C-suite. Ask them to audit your existing CRM system to determine which available visitor intelligence technologies could be integrated with minimal costs and maximum business value.

Step 2 – Select a visitor intelligence technology provider. Ask them for a trial period so that you can validate and compare your Google Analytics dashboard data to their newly provided analytics. During this trial period, verify that the contact information provided about corporate visitors is accurate and up-to-date.

Step 3 – Create a strategic dashboard, and profile the most important data points, mapping out an efficient process to get the intelligence to the right hands so that it is fresh, actionable, and relevant. People in sales are often annoyed at their colleagues in marketing because they feel they waste their time with vague data. This is a chance to prove them wrong by providing hot leads in real time.

Step 4 – Engage the entire C-suite and share the top-line reports to demonstrate the measurable value that your marketing department provides as the activated pulse of the new information age.

INSIGHTS: JENIFER KERN, V.P. OF MARKETING, CELERITY

With the right leadership, change can happen quickly. Here's a good case study of how a company got activated and took its marketing automation program from "zero to hero" in less than two years.

As vice president of marketing at Celerity, a leading digital consultancy focused on business acceleration; Jenifer Kern drives the company's sustained growth and sophistication through lead generation, digital marketing, creative branding, and sales enablement. She partners with the CEO, COO, and leadership team to guide the strategic vision of the company while ensuring competitive differentiation and business value.

When Jenifer arrived at Celerity in 2011, there was no marketing function. C-suite leadership was looking for more efficient ways to drive sales growth without making significant financial investments. They also wanted marketing to help unify the brand and develop more compelling, consistent messaging.

Once the rebrand was complete, Jenifer's next challenge was to see how they could get the brand out to the broadest marketplace using digital channels in a low-cost and efficient manner. Early in her online search, she stumbled across Eloqua and marketing automation software. She began researching the capabilities and the pros and cons of marketing automation. Simultaneously she checked out traditional advertising (promo, print, digital) and other possible brand building strategies. But with little appetite for large dollar investments, and marketing a young, unproven function within the organization, she veered back to marketing automation as a means for getting Celerity's brand message and value proposition out to the largest audience at the lowest cost.

Jenifer spent two months researching top market options: Eloqua, Marketo, SilverPop, and HubSpot. In 2012, she selected Eloqua.

But wait. The company's CRM had only 4,000 names in it with email addresses, and most were old, unverified names. In addition, only a few sales reps were conversant with the CRM, and many were tracking lead activity using other tools. How was

Celerity going to launch marketing automation with a sales team that was not fully active in the CRM and an unknown small quantity of "leads" in the database?

Jenifer went back to basics. She got to know the people in sales—the sales VPs and sales reps. How were they doing business? Were they using digital channels? Where was the intellectual sales capital of the company being kept? Jenifer brought these simple propositions to the CEO. They looked at CRM spending and utilization, and they knew that there was potential for improvement. They knew they needed adoption of CRM before marketing automation would work. They launched "Mission CRM Adoption." The reward for adoption would be marketing automation. If sales used the CRM, they would get access to new leads and could track all their leads with digital engagement, seeing prospects who opened emails and visited the website. That sounded pretty cool. The sales team got to know their new friends, Salesforce.com and Eloqua.

The company tested campaigns, starting small. In the second campaign, they got their first click-through. Bam! A sales rep called immediately. They got a qualified deal, a buyer ready to purchase. Within a few months, it was a new client. It had been the right message, at the time, to the right person. Fast sales follow-up. A pretty simple formula—"It's a numbers game," their COO loves to say.

Full disclosure: the sales rep did have a prior relationship with the buyer, but that was okay; a new deal is a new deal.

Over their first year running marketing automation, they tested campaigns from one rep, from all reps, large, small, personalized, depersonalized—all kinds of "unsophisticated" campaigns from an Eloqua standpoint. Simple click-throughs to the Celerity website, case studies, and blogs. Simple, straightforward messaging around their services, value, and some "consulting thought leadership" content. Marketing coordinated closely with sales reps on each and every campaign. We then proceeded to send them "engaged leads" (multiple openers and click-throughs) and encouraged quick follow-up in a fairly traditional manual process.

That first year, some new doors opened, with small wins. While the CEO felt it was working, he was still looking for payback on their investment. The sales team was energized, working with marketing, more supported, more confident, with more tools as CRM adoption was rising slowly and steadily.

During the second year, the marketing team became more sophisticated with a stellar content marketing strategy. They began reusing content for campaigns and developed a strong blogging platform and social media branding. The company hired a young, smart content marketer to generate content. Next, they brought in a marketing ops specialist with Eloqua background to "tame the beast"—that is, the artist formerly known as Eloqua (now Oracle), which had grown to over 40,000 names and was running eight campaigns per month.

Marketing automation was the backbone of the digital marketing engine. Deals were starting to pile up... no longer all of them small deals.

Less than two years after starting the program, they won their first major, multi-year contract, sourced solely through marketing tools (lead gen) and email nurturing campaigns—coupled with tenacious sales follow up after each campaign.

The company was looking to mature, repeat, and scale. The marketing ops specialist launched lead scoring. The fancy "Sirius Decisions" waterfall was within reach. After less than two years the pipeline was chock full of marketing sourced, marketing-influenced, and marketing-nurtured deals. It was time to get serious, start base lining, figuring out their own best practices, what was working, and how was it working. It was not just "spray and pray" anymore—they wanted to take it to the next level.

Sales turnover went way down. Reps were staying longer and getting successful faster. Celerity was in the digital business and they were practicing what they preached.

From a corporate/CEO perspective, revenues continued to increase and margins increased—which is the best possible combination. Gauging the impact of brand perception was difficult, but marketing automation makes it easier to point to collaborative sales-marketing wins. The sales VPs were less stressed and more confident with a savvy marketing team supporting them. The C-suite was impressed with the immense amount accomplished by a three-person marketing team on a limited budget.

For Jenifer, "Done is better than perfect." There's always so much more to do, more heights to reach for, which is what makes digital marketing the coolest, most challenging and invigorating field to be in right now. She will never be done. Lovable imperfection is her best friend. And while marketing automation has helped her drive success, she still claims "there's no silver bullet in marketing ... multi-channel, multi-touch is always the best approach."

FACTS YOU NEED TO KNOW

▶ **Amazon says that 35% of its product sales result from its recommendation engines.**

▶ **"49% of marketers identify capturing and integrating customer data as being a key consideration."**

▶ **"Marketing automation is inherently designed to go after new customers."**

CHAPTER 10
LOOK BEFORE YOU LEAP: MARKETING AUTOMATION ISN'T FOOLPROOF

Let's return, if we may, to the faraway kingdom of Emperor Ceo. In our story, the con artists Slick & Shark were exposed, their crummy work rejected, and the clothing contract canceled. A great sigh of relief could be heard throughout the kingdom.

Emperor Ceo didn't want the same disaster to happen twice. No one was going to fool him again! He had heard about the magical elixir called "marketing automation." He had heard that this amazing stuff was easy to use, maintenance-free, and would guarantee that the emperor got the information that he needed to make wise decisions.

The word "automation" was what intrigued him. It suggested a perpetual motion machine: you just set it up, turn it on, and it runs all by itself. What could be better?

Throughout the kingdom, a call went out for a vendor who could provide Emperor Ceo with marketing automation.

As it happened, while Slick & Shark had been banished, the devious duo were still living under assumed names in a distant suburb of the empire. Hearing the call, they traveled to the capital and presented themselves as Quick & Quack. "Your Highness," they told the emperor, "We can give you exactly what you want. Our marketing automation software is at the cutting edge of digital technology. You can set it and forget it! Gone are the days of messy human interaction. Gone are those unreliable front-line people who want things like coffee breaks and vacations. Nowadays it's all done with electrons. Fast and cheap."

Need we say more? Emperor Ceo was snookered again. He bought the expensive marketing automation package from Quick & Quack. The duo set it up, and this time they were smarter: they left town with their bag of cash. They were last seen lying on a white sand beach on an island far away, sipping unnaturally colored rum drinks.

While marketing automation is the undeniable wave of the future, like any powerful tool you have to know how to use it. It is not set-it-and-forget-it. At the end of the day, for your business to grow and thrive, it's a matter of your people, from the live chat operator to your chairman of the board.

INSIGHTS: DAVID E. TAYLOR, JR., SVP OF MARKETING & SALES AT KAJEET

As the senior vice president of marketing and sales at Kajeet, the leading provider of mobile broadband solutions for kids and educational institutions, Dave Taylor drives revenue by developing and executing strategic business development programs and providing hands-on leadership, guidance, and management of the marketing, communications, sales, and branding functions. Dave is responsible for building long term and sustainable relationships with Kajeet's primary customer groups: K-12 educational institutions and direct consumers.

He's got plenty of people experience, having directed departments as large as fifty staff members and as small as four. In terms of influence, in his role as a sales and marketing executive, he interacts and influences various departments including product development, account/client management, and operations.

Sorting through today's sea of digital business tools to find the ones that are worth investing in comes down to discipline and making the effort to carve out a certain amount of time each day, or each week, to weed through all the Google Alerts, Twitter feeds, and LinkedIn updates. Technology is extremely helpful in allowing a professional to ensure that information they are interested in is conveniently pushed to them. However, the difficulty is finding time to really digest the information while still being productive.

It's easy to get lost in the digital tsunami and forget the human element. Dave sees that email, texting, and instant messaging too often become crutches that people hide behind because they lack the ability to verbally express ideas, thoughts, and opinions. He has noticed that younger employees especially, can find it difficult to develop the skills required to master the art of the in-person presentation. Texting is spawning a whole generation of professionals who do not understand the art of professional business communication, because to them, everything comes in 140-character sound bites and fragmented sentences.

Technology is too easy to hide behind. As you embrace technology, you must also hold an attitude of "back to the future." In a world of email, Skype, texting, and instant message, Dave still finds the most effective way of communicating is the same as it was in the twentieth century: in-person, face-to-face, two-way, dialog. The written word (or face-less verbal communication) can only utilize a small part of the full "communication spectrum." Body language (of both the giver and receiver), gesturing, whiteboarding, subtle facial expressions, and good ole' fashioned rapport-building round out the full spectrum of communication. These are things that can only truly be conveyed in person. Without the ability to utilize the full spectrum of communication, you can only emote part of your intended communication.

The biggest challenges with leveraging technology have more to do with the people than the technology itself. Dave finds that individuals often become enamored with the promise of the technology, or the automation ability of the technology, and this can lead to less preparation and planning in the use of that technology. Regardless of the technology platform that is used, he still has a "pre-flight" checklist for his staff that they review before each and every campaign is launched.

Dave's preferred method of communication is in person. Phone is the last resort. He uses email all day long, but in a situation where you have to exchange a dozen emails to simply agree to understanding an outcome of the original message is just insane; stop by the recipient's office or pick up the phone. He uses text more and more but only for quick, non-critical things like "running 5 min late for meeting," "R U in your office?"

Having said that, digital communications are an incredibly powerful tool. Email is a critical part of anybody's workday. Not only does it allow you to communicate with one or many people all at once (albeit using only a small portion of the communication spectrum), it is also a terrific tool for storing and recalling past conversation strings that you just can't do in many other ways. To leverage this potential, Dave has created an elaborate file storage structure for his email and developed a number of rules to help him manage email more as a data repository than as a communication tool.

Dave measures everything. As he says, "You can take the boy out of database marketing, but you can't take the database marketing out of the boy." Everything can be measured if properly planned and constructed to do so. Over the years, he's been fortunate to use many high-end data mining, results engine, and predictive modeling tools. There is no substitute for them when you have hundreds (or thousands) of campaigns, audience segments, and test cells to dig through. But sometimes, his greatest satisfaction comes from sitting down with a simple, yet often-overlooked tool like Microsoft Excel. He finds great satisfaction crunching small- to mid-size data sets, utilizing functions, and letting one of the greatest inventions of our time—Pivot Tables—work its magic. It is amazing how much more you can learn when you become intimately engaged with the data again, and are not simply reading reports or gazing at dashboards.

Dave uses social media, especially SM. He began way back in the day when no one knew if it was effective or how to use it. Was it valuable, could it drive sales? Now he's seeing quite a bit of benefit from brand reinforcement, customer communication, goodwill, and, best for last, sales lead generation. It actually does work. It only took almost a decade to figure that out, but it works! For Dave, Twitter, LinkedIn, and industry-related sites work best. Facebook and YouTube not so much, but that's just his current industry and market.

When getting into marketing automation, you select the right vendor (the first time) and be sure to understand how to inexpensively and completely configure the system to work seamlessly with your legacy systems. Then, ensure that your employees understand, and can take advantage of, the full range of functionality of a marketing automation tool. Then you'll really have something.

Looking ahead, Dave thinks someone will figure out "big data" and how it can really be applied to increase business and drive revenue. It sort of feels like social media did in the first decade of this century; everyone is talking about it, but most don't know what it really means for them.

He thinks that the consumer will continue to move up stream in the buying cycle and that sales staff will need to learn to become trusted advisors rather than traditional sales people. Social will continue to grow and become a bigger part of a company brand strategy—maybe even the primary challenge in managing a brand.

It's about the soul of the company and how that conveys in the intent of your communications. Social media has made all of us very astute students of BS detection. Insincerity is very transparent, while sincerity and good intentions always shine through.

THREE ETERNAL TRUTHS

Gerard E. Sample, who provided insights earlier in the book, echoes the idea that despite new technologies—which you need to embrace—there are three eternal truths regardless of where you are in the number and evolution of communication mediums.

The first is to be authentic, credible, and relevant. These have always been, and will continue to be, the most important attributes of any communication philosophy or campaign. If you are coming in as a leader and you see that those items are generally lacking, it's incumbent upon you to lead through example in order to effect that change.

Second, you have to provide the training, tools and encouragement to help everyone within the organization grow individually. In raising the watermark collectively, you increase the communication self-awareness of the whole organization, which will translate into cultural change and greater customer efficacy.

Third, someone new to the organization should, even if it's internal, do a pretty thoughtful assessment of who the personas are within that organization like we do from an outbound perspective. What's the profile? If I'm taking over the mainframe team it's going to be a very different team to catch than taking over the marcom team. And in doing that, you have to be cognizant and start at a point where you're not going to instantly alienate everyone, but you can take iterative steps to evolve the richness, relevance, and credibility of their communication abilities.

CHAPTER 11
EMPLOYER BRANDING

After the twin debacles of Slick & Shark and Quick & Quack, Emperor Ceo realized that he needed to hire new people to help him run his kingdom. The citizens were mocking him, his army was not meeting its quota of lands conquered, and the kingdom's products were languishing on the shelves. In short, the kingdom's brand had taken a hit. Emperor Ceo wanted desperately to turn the kingdom around. He knew he couldn't do it alone.

The call went out: the kingdom was hiring. Plenty of good positions were available to be filled by the best and the brightest. Administrative, marketing, finance, communications—every department had the directive to recruit fresh talent.

At last, thought Emperor Ceo, his troubles would soon be behind him, and he could go back to his golf game without suffering further anxiety.

A week after the jobs were posted on Merlin's List, the emperor summoned his duke of human resources.

"Tell me, duke, have all the positions been filled?" asked the emperor.

"Um, not exactly," replied the duke of HR.

"What?" thundered the emperor. "What's the problem? We're offering outstanding pay and benefits. We're even giving each new hire a thousand gold coins as a signing bonus!"

"Yes, Your Highness, our compensation is indeed most generous," replied the duke of HR. "But for some reason we're not getting the qualified applicants that we expected."

"If I may interrupt," said the baron of communications, who had been loitering in the throne room, "perhaps I can explain."

"Okay," said the emperor. "Explain!"

"What we're hearing on social media is that our employer brand is very poor."

"Employer brand?" said the emperor. "What the devil is that? Isn't our consumer brand strong?"

"Yes, Your Highness," replied the baron of communications. "Our consumer brand is strong. Employer branding is different. It has to do with how we're perceived from the outside when we're recruiting people. The term 'employer branding' was coined about twenty years ago by Simon Barrow, chairman of People in Business, and Tim Ambler, Senior Fellow of London Business School, in the *Journal of Brand Management*. Within this paper, Barrow and Ambler defined the employer brand as 'the package of functional, economic and psychological benefits provided by employment, and identified with the employing company.'

"For example," continued the baron, "most kingdoms think of their website as a marketing tool. It's a way to sell products to people and collect revenues. Likewise, they think of social media as a way to influence public opinion and get consumer feedback. But in reality these channels also contribute to their recruitment brand. Our employer brand is how we're perceived by a specialized segment of the market—namely, the talented people who might want to work here. If we have a lousy employer brand, we're going to attract lousy candidates who can't get hired anywhere else."

"Come to think of it," said the emperor, "My new official food taster is a lousy hire. The guy can't even tell the difference between arsenic and hemlock. I'm going to fire him."

"We had to hire him because no one else applied for the job," interjected the duke of HR.

"I've heard about a new process for turning around an organization," mused the emperor. "It's called getting activated. Does it work?"

"To get activated," said the baron of communications, "means that you leverage the power of digital communications in all of its forms to increase productivity, transparency, agility, and accountability. Increased profits surely follow. Nowadays, the best and brightest candidates expect a kingdom to be activated. If you're not, they think you're hopelessly old-fashioned."

"Like a dinosaur," quipped the duke of HR.

"Is this anything like what Quick & Quack sold us?" asked the emperor.

"No," replied the baron. "Those guys were just software peddlers. They had no clue about the bigger picture, and how the human element is still the most important thing."

"How does employer branding get created within the organization?" asked the emperor.

"Call it internal marketing," said the baron. "The focus is on communicating the customer brand promise, and the performance expected from employees to deliver on that promise. It is beneficial to the organization for employees to understand their role in delivering the customer brand promise; and to be effective, the service experience must be experienced by the employees in their interactions with the organization. To close any gap, employer brand thinking and practice may spur a more mutually beneficial employment deal."

"Okay," said Emperor Ceo. "Let's get activated. Let's do what we have to do to ensure that our employer brand is both attractive and competitive with that of any other kingdom. I want the very best people working here. I want them to be productive and happy. I want low employee turnover, and I want the kingdom to be known far and wide as being a great place to work."

ORGANIZATIONAL SELF-EVALUATION

Leaders like Emperor Ceo often say, "Our people are our greatest assets," or, "Our best assets walk out every night and return in the morning." Most chief executives really mean it when they say it. They sincerely believe that their greatest human capital is composed of the passionate and hardworking people they see in the office each day.

But on more than one occasion, many firms find it extremely difficult to look at themselves from the "outside in." Most firms find it challenging to objectively evaluate how the organization may look to prospective candidates who are searching for an innovative company with a thriving culture to call home.

How do you look from the outside in? Successful companies take the time to ask themselves some hard questions and often invite a strategic third party to test and validate their perceptions. After all, if you look in your own mirror, you're only going to see yourself the way you always have.

Here are six warning signs that indicate that your recruitment brand needs to get activated.

▶ When asked, "What is the company's vision?" your employees answer, "What vision?"

▶ When asked, "Describe your company culture," your employees answer, "Put in your hours and keep your mouth shut."

▶ Your leadership team emphasizes "innovation" as a core value in corporate marketing materials, but the conference room where you interview candidates looks like the year 1986, with an overhead projector running on Windows XP.

▶ Your website's career section includes job descriptions and requisite numbers but does not offer any compelling description of why your company is a great place to work.

▶ Your best employees do not feel comfortable referring their friends to your company because they don't want friends to become enemies after having a bad experience.

▶ Your social media channels such as Facebook and Twitter have no organic followers, other than the obligatory HR representatives who post new job openings.

Employer branding is a framework for defining, managing, and communicating the total employment relationship with both current and prospective employees. The key is to align the organization's image with the employee experience so that organizational messages are consistent with actions. The messages created in the values, systems, policies and behaviors of the organization should all be in alignment.

As with reputation, the employer brand will happen whether or not the organization acts to enhance it, so it is better to be proactive to shape the employer brand rather than let it just grow uncontrolled. Successful employer branding is built on the employer's ability to deliver on its promise, and when this happens the organization becomes a place that attracts the best and brightest candidates.

Employer branding is about a total approach to the employee experience, and doesn't focus merely on short-term feel-good efforts or tokenism. It is not about t-shirts, slogans, logos, inscribed coffee mugs, company mouse pads, recruitment advertising campaigns, or training programs on the external brand. While such collateral may be used in employer branding campaigns, it needs to be both apt and relevant. A positive employer brand is built over time, and must be consistent and verified by testimony on social media.

What's the most effective way to overtly communicate your employer brand? When it comes to internal communications in corporate America, gone are the days of the office memo that drifted down from the C-suite to the lower floors. The formal rules and boundaries of what, when, and how we communicate (between employees, middle management, and the C-suite) have dissolved as digital communication technologies such as instant messaging (IM), Twitter, Instagram, email, and other forms of social media have blurred the lines.

Here's an overview of the top digital communications tools that can help shape your organization's employer brand, and the pros and cons of each:

INTERNAL COMMUNICATIONS TOOL	WHY IT IS GOOD	WHY IT IS BAD
Instant Messaging (IM)	Getting an easy question answered. Fast and to the point. It's like texting with a keyboard.	Getting an important question answered. Easy to get sidetracked when IM is always on. People know if you are available or not.
Face to Face Meetings	Hashing out responsibilities and project duties. Face to face meetings help employees get messaging and strategy clear.	Can be time consuming.
Phone Conversations	Reaching someone who is out of the office. Great for quick request and offers a person's "tone" that digital communication lacks.	Reaching someone who is in the office. It's up to the users to document anything that came out of the conversation. No digital trail.
Email	Sharing detailed information with large groups of people (or even small groups). Communication chains are easily tracked in email.	Arguing different opinions. Most employees already get a 1,000 annoying emails.
Text Messaging	Great for emergencies.	Poor way to check on progress of projects. Can be overused for non-emergencies.
Social Media (LinkedIn, Facebook, Scoop It)	Great for sharing information with large groups. You can typically find the person you are looking for at just about any time.	Bad for sharing private company knowledge. It's in public view.
Corporate Intranet (SharePoint, Yammer, SalesForce.com)	Great for widely distributing priorities. Catalogues both conversations and files associated with them.	Bad for completing said priorities. Employees have to log in and make 20 clicks before something is sent.
Voice Mail	Great for leaving information for someone who isn't available. Also works well when you are driving and have a lot to say.	Bad for expecting someone to call you back (that's what email is for). Documentation of your request/conversation is only saved on one side.

INSIGHTS: EMPLOYER BRANDING ROUND TABLE

We recently asked a select group of top communications executives to answer some questions about employer branding. And what better place to make it interactive than conducting the discussion online, live, raw, on the very active LinkedIn's robust International Association of Business Communicators Forum boasting over 36,000 members.

For our first question, we asked them to comment on what they saw as the three most important barriers to success in communicating with employees, comparing the 1990s to today.

Paula Lammey, Director Corporate Communication and Community at Ausenco Limited

I'm not sure if it's changed between the nineties and now, but I would have to say the top barriers to success in communicating with employees are these:

▶ Leaders who don't see the value in communicating well to their teams (i.e., they don't see it as one of their priorities).

▶ People managers who don't have the skills or support systems to communicate with their people.

▶ Communication that is too "corporate" and doesn't meet employees' needs. It doesn't explain what the message means for them or what they should do with the information they receive.

Mike Jenkins, Communications Director, College of Arts and Letters at Michigan State University

Here are three barriers to success in communicating with employees:

▶ Leaders who say one thing and do the opposite (usually in a bad way), such as say their door is always open and they have no ego when they display a huge one on a daily basis.

▶ Communications vehicles or platforms that are not the way that employees want to receive or are willing to receive their communication.

▶ Communications that do not reflect the organizational culture, and are not what employees want or need to hear or know.

The true barriers haven't changed that much, except that we now have hundreds of choices in TV and competing programming. People also choose how they want to receive information, and we need to identify and honor their wishes and respect their time and intelligence where we can.

Then we asked our Round Table, "Do social media outlets such as Facebook, Twitter, and even instant messaging help or hurt?"

Mike Jenkins

Whether social media outlets such as Facebook, Twitter, and even instant messaging help or hurt depends on where your employees are on social media platforms and accounts, IM and chat, and if they respond to and with it, and how. Also, whether they even want their employer to "connect" with them on what they consider "their" social media accounts and/or platforms. As you probably know, many employees don't want their employers getting too personal. (Or acting hip, or "with it," when they aren't.)

Joy Niemerg, Communications Strategist—Dedicated to Creating Effective Communications Plans to Meet Business Objectives

Whether social media outlets such as Facebook, Twitter, and even instant messaging help or hurt, I would say this:

- Employees are now hit in so many directions with messaging that it is often very difficult to get their attention.

- Getting management to realize that the world has changed and what used to work, doesn't work anymore. Employees are not as loyal now. They want to feel appreciated and be talked to like human beings.

- Big business is often too focused on the stakeholders and not the employees. As a result, messaging tends to sound more like directives and less like sharing and working as a team.

I've mostly worked with very large, conservative companies, so this may not apply to everyone.

Margaret Airs, Arkimedia Creative Communications Ltd.

You asked for the three barriers. They are attitude, perception, and complexity.

We then asked if they saw age as a barrier within this context. For example, some say that Millennials communicate differently than Gen-X and so forth. Does that impact their views about employer branding?

Carolyn Ballou, Communications Director

I'd add employee mindset to the mix. I have worked in environments in which an "us against them" perspective is deeply ingrained in employees. They are suspect of any communication from organization leaders, and are resistant to legitimate attempts by managers to engage.

Richard Lomax, Director, Beetroot

The biggest barrier today is not age as much as it is the vast and growing salary gap between top and bottom. Unless and until staff see this trend reversing, all calls for more discretionary effort, pride and engagement aimed at boosting profits ring hollow.

Christopher J. Kramer, Manager Media Relations at Argonne National Laboratory

In prior organizations I worked I sometimes found that leadership's concept of communication was, "We tell them what we want them to know." I remember in one organization I worked at years ago, the leadership hired a consultant to find out what was wrong with internal communication. After many surveys, interviews, and questions, the consultant told leadership that, in fact, it was the leadership that was the primary communication problem. They only pushed information out and never listened to the staff. In response, the leadership promptly fired the consultant! Nothing changed until the agency director was eventually replaced with someone who was willing to listen to staff. So, in my humble opinion, one of the greatest barriers to employee communication is not providing easy-to-use channels for constructive employee ideas and feedback. You need to actually listen to what your employees—and your expensive consultants—are telling you.

Nicole McPhee, Communications & Change Management

I find all the platforms that are out there don't hurt. In fact, it helps me communicate with my audience better, as I have options for the various audiences.

I work at a college, so my audience is the students as well as the employees. I know what they prefer, and I post accordingly. Students get fun and informative posts on Facebook and Twitter, whereas employees prefer to get their posts on Twitter and LinkedIn. But with both I try to increase engagement by asking them questions and for their opinions on pictures/videos/links.

John Thompson, Speechwriter, Strategic Communication Consultant, Adjunct Professor of Business

By far, the number one issue I see is that many executives do not see communications as part of the skill set required; it is viewed as a "nice to have." That speaks to organizational culture as well. For the modern leader, communications has to be seen on an equal footing as operational management and financial acumen. Since you asked for three, let's add missing out on the basics of audience analysis and considering the real purpose of communications.

Sherree Geyer, Strategic Public Relations, Marketing Communications, Social Media, Writer with Expertise in Healthcare

Employees can be the biggest advocates of an organization. If a corporation has a presence online (and they should), employees should be encouraged to visit the company intranet/website and keep up on social media chatter on Facebook and Twitter. As a former communications manager, I used to send an internal email to all employees encouraging them to check out a new press release posted to our website. Employees can often correct misinformation spread by social media pages and should be encouraged to use corporate communications as a gateway for this type of feedback. We live in a transparent media world. To attempt to control access to information the way we did thirty years ago is futile and can lead to misinformation.

Lori Arkin-Diem, Communications Manager, InterContinental Hotels Group

I see the first barrier as too many emails and other communication venues coming at the reader at the same time. Second is people not being strategic about when and what they communicate. This contributes to barrier number one.

My number three is actually a solution that is mentioned in other comments. Talk to your audience. Find out what they want to know (the gaps in their employee experience) and take a poll on how they like to receive information. Once you follow through, follow-up regularly and ask how you are hitting the mark.

Rob Sims, Communications Professional Focused on Life Science Learning Technology

My experience tells me that barrier number one is a transient mentality. Many knowledge workers don't envision their position as long term, resulting in minimum engagement and a lack of enthusiasm to digest useful, actionable content.

Barrier two is "reinforced silos." We as communicators need to break down department silos, given the increase in outsourcing and remote employees. This can be done by putting on our KM hats, sharing operational conversations, project wins, and best practices.

Barrier three is one-way communication. I don't think we solicit enough feedback about what folks really need to get things done better and faster, while developing as professionals.

Anna Neale, Senior Advisor, Corporate Communications at EPCOR

I'm not sure about the United States or other countries, but in Canada there is a lot of PR / comms work, so employees are less loyal now, they are in more demand, and they have more jobs to choose from. I think employees today are also generally less engaged. Combine these two factors with a much stronger expectation by employees for employers to actively engage, and I mean authentically engage them, not just "offer a robust employee engagement program" (because we all know employee engagement isn't a program or a box that can be checked), and you have some significant, but I believe, manageable barriers to effectively communicate with and importantly, be heard by, your employees.

José Romero, Internal Communications at Randstad

First, people don't like to read. If you don't keep up the texts with graphics or make short texts (linked to intranet), you are not going to catch their attention.

Second, managers who think "communication" means "just forward an email" are laggards for the corporation's communications.

Third, and last but not least, there is a lot of focus on corporate communications and less focus on employee engagement and on the real needs of communications of our staff. And communication is the most effective way to gain the engagement of the people.

Cindy Alfaro, Analista de Comunicación

I believe that the barriers may be different according to the perspective, industry, culture and work environment. However, I'll mention the following:

▶ Lack or absence of planning and good leadership. Remember that holding a hierarchical, superior position does not make someone a leader.

▶ Resistance to change, lack of corporate identity, diminished employee loyalty to the company, and the constant pursuit of personal and professional improvement. There will always be something better, so it is necessary to have a mixed and effective communication structure.

▶ Using communication only as an information channel, without connecting to the receiver, the message, and the organization. No feedback is generated when there is fear of negative criticism from the company or reprisals against employees. Any negative or positive criticism is constructive.

▶ Information overload. An excessive flow of data limits the understanding of the message and the assessment of information from the perspective of employees, and results in a lack of interest in what is being communicated.

Tara Mooney, Global Communications Consultant

Here are two barriers:

▶ A tendency to forget that one of the main benefits of internal communications is its capacity to improve relationships between all people, no matter how transient their jobs, which then translates to their reduced stress and a range of other performance improvements.

▶ Leaders and staff are too slow to change behaviors and embrace informal, short, face-to-face chats and webcams as a way of life.

There is still an over-reliance on the written word channeled through broadcasts (email, internet, etc.) and on face-to-face gatherings that take up too much time, leaving employees stressed. If corporations could just embrace webcams and webcasts a little more, relationships would improve, engagement would skyrocket, and time-consuming emails and meetings would reduce!

Manon Cote, Owner at En Communication

Companies often see communications as a one-way street and forget to ask for feedback. They do not keep consistent messaging, and they send tons of emails or intranet articles and think that they've communicated.

Richard House, International Director, Nextar Communications

Traditionally the emphasis has been on messaging—"What to say," and later on "How to say it"—narrative. Now we see "who to be" (persona) emerging as an important component of effective communication. That's the hard one!

Donna Autuori, President, Autuori Corporate Communications, Inc.

I believe it starts with executives and managers not recognizing just how important open, two-way communications are in keeping employees engaged, motivated, productive, and even loyal. It's unfortunate that in many businesses employees are discouraged from voicing their opinions or offering suggestions that often would lead to improved results for the business. The solution is to enlighten leaders about the benefits that effective communications bring to the workplace.

Lisa Marie Bast, Public & Media Relations I Corporate Communications I Internal Communications I Marketing Communications

Effective employee communications, I believe, starts with a people-centric culture. If employees don't feel the organization values them—their opinions, feedback, and contributions—then any attempt at employee communications will fail over the long term. Organization must first promote a people-centric environment, which will lay the groundwork for effective employee communications.

Pauline Nelson, Principal at Pauline S. Nelson & Associates

Breaking down barriers and achieving greater transparency means having:

▶ Good leaders who understand and appreciate the importance of effective communication.

▶ The readiness and attitude of employees to receive and participate in the process.

▶ The channels and tools used in the process.

Heather Bussey, Change Leadership Through Strategic Communications Excellence

1. As professional communicators, we need to avoid getting sucked into the social media vortex. These are vehicles, just like any newsletter, poster or brochure. Look at the five Ws that span the business objective and audience needs, and then add the How.

2. There is an over-use of employee engagement surveys as empty gestures. Communications professionals need to take the lead with HR and internal clients to ensure a post-survey action plan is developed and communicated to employees in a way that shows them they were heard and what they can expect. Continue to update employees on organizational progress in addressing the key drivers. Don't waste money on another survey until you can say with confidence that you have addressed the major drivers.

3. Clean house first, then measure. Do you need to spend money to create a benchmark based on current poor performance? Employees generally are driven by the same things: a) Clear career pathing and development opportunities. b) An environment that supports wellness and work/home balance. This includes respect for time and also a comprehensive benefits package. Don't make the mistake of calling this latter feature out as distinct from the overall wellness and balance theme. c) Having the tools to get the job done. d) Transparent and honest communications from leaders and supervisors.

Don't be distracted by results that say, "Feeling like I am being heard" is a driver. Pay is important, but is not necessarily a driver to engagement in the face of other conditions. It took a backseat years ago with the economic downturn. It's all about empowering employees to stay agile and resilient to workplace change, and providing a decent place to work.

Be honest and avoid surprises. Expect the best and enable it to happen. Be brave. Get rid of the toxic folks, including managers and leaders. Excellent results are not worth the message you are perpetuating. Postpone the survey and spend that money on coaching, training, and equipping your employees, and ensuring your managers and leaders have the leadership competencies and communications skills your people are looking for. Then measure yourself against the organizations in your industry who already have it right.

Judy Hackett, Chief Marketing Officer, Dun & Bradstreet Credibility Corp.

Hire entrepreneurial employees and nurture a culture of entrepreneurism. As an example, in our office we have a Failure Wall. You screw up, you put it on the wall. Eventually, the failure fades away. We learn more from our failures than our successes. It gets pretty easy for employees to take risks and learn to turn on a dime when this is inherent in your company culture.

CHAPTER 12
ONLINE REPUTATION MANAGEMENT

Having improved the kingdom's employer brand, Emperor Ceo was able to hire and retain the top talent in the kingdom. With a great sense of relief, he headed to the Monarch Golf Club for a leisurely eighteen holes.

As he was teeing up, his golf buddy, King Boardchair, was casually surfing the web on his phone.

"Have you seen this?" said the king.

"Have I seen what?" grumbled the emperor.

"When I Google 'kingdom,' one of the top results is a tabloid story about Slick & Shark. It's all about how you got snookered. Looks like you're the laughingstock of the Monarch Club."

"That happened months ago!" complained the emperor.

"And look at this," said King Boardchair. "The YouTube video of you parading around in your birthday suit has racked up seven hundred million hits! You're ready to surpass 'Charlie Bit My Finger' as one of the top videos of all time!"

"That's not good," replied the emperor. "Okay—I'll put together a team to manage our online reputation."

What do people see when they Google your business? The first page of search results is your one shot at a good first impression, so if the answer isn't "great things," then you have a serious problem. The Internet gives everyone a voice, so it's important that the loudest ones have good things to say about you.

It's not just a matter of getting rid of the bad stuff. Even the lack of online content can be damaging to your reputation, because you will not appear as credible or relevant as your activated competitors.

If you are the president, CEO, or other prominent business executive, the search results for your name are just as important to your organization's image as the results for its name. And if you're an employee, your online reputation plays a massive role in your ability to advance in your career.

Unfortunately, most people have no idea of the extent to which their online reputation can be shaped. Although you cannot delete other voices from the Internet, you can take steps to be the loudest one. Every business is faced with risks that stem from the free flow of information. Even things that aren't true can hurt you. A comprehensive online reputation management strategy can mitigate many of these risks, but it takes time and dedication to implement successfully. Here are a few tips to get started.

Publish content of your own. Sure you have a website and maybe a Facebook page, but how often are they updated? New, quality content published weekly is excellent for SEO and necessary to reach the top results. Dominate the first page of search engines and drown out other voices by posting relevant content to Facebook, Twitter, LinkedIn, Tumblr, SlideShare and WordPress. Just don't post fluff. Search engines ignore it, and people see right through it. But they will share content that is relevant to them, which amplifies your voice.

Remain informed about what people are saying about you. Google has long offered a service called Google Alerts that emails you when new information containing a selected search term is published. You may have even been advised to create one for your name or business. However, Google has admitted that this tool no longer functions the way it was intended. Superior resources such as Talkwalker.com should be used to monitor what is being posted about you and your company

Respond to negative comments. Maybe someone has given your business an unfavorable review on Yelp or GlassDoor, or posted a complaint or a frustrated tweet for the world to see. Promptly respond with an apology or explanation and offer to remedy the situation. Your response will be visible alongside the negative post, and viewers will be able to see that you care about your customers.

IF YOU'RE NOT ON LINKEDIN, YOU DON'T EXIST

Imagine a world where people have to meet face-to-face by paying an exorbitant amount of money to attend an event where they might meet one or two qualified subject matter experts. Add into the mix travel and loss of productivity associated with attendance, and you'll be spending big bucks! Now open your eyes and thank the gods of LinkedIn, the company that changed the way we do business. While LinkedIn may have started as a career-networking site, to many executives it has quickly become a valuable strategic asset. I don't mind telling people that I owe some of my best professional networking contacts to the humble beginnings of a "connect request" on LinkedIn.

When used correctly, LinkedIn is one of the single most competitive tools that an executive can hold in his or her professional arsenal. Yet, every day, I meet executives who still profess that they don't want anyone to see their connections. Good luck with that, dinosaurs. I can Google you and find out where you live via Google Earth in seconds, and pinpoint your association membership in minutes. This could result in a less-than-favorable brand presentation, considering you did not control the message.

Fortunately, these following tips can help you take advantage of LinkedIn and empower you to proactively control how the world sees you, the executive with a distinct personal brand, and you, the ambassador of your corporate brand.

1. YOUR PROFILE CONTENT DEFINES YOUR ONLINE REPUTATION

Treat your personal LinkedIn profile as if you had one opportunity to make a first impression on your target audience. Ask yourself, what do I want other executives, media reporters, and prospective employers to know about me? How do I want to be positioned? For example, you might be a mid-level manager or a chief executive officer, but failing to identify your industry expertise, credentials and certifications are a sure way of devaluing your own brand online.

2. YOUR PROFILE PICTURE IS WORTH 100,000 WORDS

If you are a business executive, make sure that your profile picture is professionally taken or professionally edited, so it doesn't look like you just graduated from college. Do not post a picture of yourself and your partner on a beach in Aruba. LinkedIn is the wrong audience, wrong intent, and wrong timing to promote your fun-loving nature. LinkedIn is a business-focused social media tool.

3. ARE YOU IN GOOD COMPANY?

From a strategic brand optics perspective, LinkedIn Profiles allow you to display that you are in "good company" or in "bad company." Choose your online associates carefully and don't accept random invitations without strategic context. My rule of thumb is this: when someone invites me, I first click on their profile, check which LinkedIn Groups they belong to, and then make an informed decision. I don't focus on evaluating our mutual connections, because I can gain more valuable insight by looking into the person's organic network.

4. CREATE MEANINGFUL CONTENT THAT POSITIONS YOU AS A STRATEGIC CONTRIBUTOR

Through content syndication, LinkedIn will add many articles to your daily read. Most of them will be tailored to your specific area of interest. This is your opportunity to show that you aren't a robot and you actually have strong professional opinions. With LinkedIn, you can share your professional opinions as long as you are using appropriate language. In fact, LinkedIn's Influencer program was inspired by the mass following that pithy critiques generate when commenting about pertinent topics in your industry.

5. DON'T FORGET TO LINK YOUR LINKEDIN AND TWITTER SOCIAL MEDIA ACCOUNTS

Not only does LinkedIn provide you with the most qualified audience of well-networked executives, but with a simple setup, you can also ensure that your best comments double up as your tweet of the day or the week, further extending your digital reach.

CHAPTER 13
LIVE IN A GLASS HOUSE? DON'T THROW DIGITAL STONES!

One day as he was relaxing in his throne room, Emperor Ceo decided that he would like a sandwich from the corner deli. He looked around to see who could go the deli and pick up a turkey club. His official taster was in the hospital recovering from acute gastroenteritis, and the usual assortment of court flunkies and sycophants were hiding. There was no one to do his bidding.

Then he spied a little boy. A page, no taller than a sapling.

"Come here, page," commanded the emperor.

"Yes?" replied the page.

"Go to the deli and get me a turkey club on whole wheat. Hold the pickle. Extra mayo. A bag of chips, too. Got it? Good. Here are five gold coins for the sandwich. And here's a gold coin for you. Now go."

Instead of hurrying away, the little boy just stood there.

"Well, what's keeping you?" thundered Emperor Ceo.

"One gold coin?" replied the page. "Are you kidding?"

"What do you mean?" said the emperor. "It's what everyone gets."

"No it's not," said the page. "Last week you paid Sir Galahad two gold coins to fetch your sandwich."

"Well, he's a knight," blustered the emperor. "He's got seniority."

"It's the same job," said the boy. "Go to deli. Get sandwich and bag of chips. Return to throne room. It should be the same pay no matter who does it."

The emperor was becoming irritated. "When I was your age," he said, "We didn't run around comparing paychecks. It was unseemly. You would never tell a coworker how much you got paid. That was private. Between you and your boss."

"Yeah," replied the page. "That worked out pretty well for the boss! Divide and conquer. You could pay different people different rates, depending on the labor market and your own biases. Those days are over, dude. I know what everyone gets paid around here. It's no big deal. It's no secret."

Emperor Ceo sighed. Just when he thought he had everything figured out, there was a new angle. A new challenge to the old order that he had to deal with. And he was hungry.

"Okay, kid," he sighed. "I'll pay you two gold coins. But don't tell anyone, okay?"

The page took the gold coins. As he ran to the deli he took out his mobile phone and posted online what he had been paid. "Sorry, Emperor Ceo," he said to himself. "This is the new world!"

As I'll say 'till my face turns blue, in today's digital marketplace, you and your company are participants in the forum of public opinion whether you like it or not. People—your customers and your employees—are exchanging ideas and comments about every facet of your business, both internally and externally. They're talking about your products and services, your human resource policies, how you are as a boss, and what it's like to interact with your company. You cannot ignore today's activated world. You need to get on top of it.

Employer branding is no longer just about what you do with people while they're in your kingdom, under your watchful eye. You've got to worry about what they say about you when they leave the kingdom as they go and post their experiences and confidential views, from praise to the anonymous bashing that collectively defines your brand.

This includes an area that used to be sacrosanct—how much people get paid.

Whether or not a company has an official policy of transparency, you can find a wealth of information about nearly any organization online. Digital corporate brand reputation management for employers lives and dies in web sites like GlassDoor.com and Careerbliss.com.

GLASSDOOR.COM

Launched in 2008, Glassdoor is an online job and career site where employees anonymously comment on both the good and bad points of their companies and bosses. The website features reviews and commentary from both current and former employees. In the year prior to April 2014, more than half a million company reviews were submitted to the site.

Glassdoor says that by using technological checks of email addresses and screenings by a content management team, it verifies that the reviews come from real employees.

By providing insider information to potential employees, Glassdoor has revolutionized the job hunt by creating more transparency in the workplace. Glassdoor helps job seekers narrow down the options and create a select group of companies that they will then consider as potential employers.

Simply having a Glassdoor profile can therefore increase an organization's visibility to job seekers, and possibly increase the number of applications.

In addition to written commentary by current and former employees, Glassdoor requires reviewers to rate the company—out of five stars—in five areas:

✓ Culture and values

✓ Work / life balance

✓ Senior management

✓ Comp and benefits

✓ Career opportunities

A survey conducted by Software Advice revealed that almost half of all survey respondents had used Glassdoor at some point in their job search. Many respondents said they use it early in the job search process. For most job seekers, positive reviews in the compensation and benefits category are most important to job seekers. Good ratings of work/life balance came in second.

Glassdoor reviewers are also asked to rate the CEO of the company.

CAREERBLISS

According to its website, CareerBliss is an "online career community and resource dedicated to helping you find joy and success at every step in your career. CareerBliss discovers the hidden influences that drive your work happiness and offers you the tools to help you unlock your bliss potential. Our goal is to make people happier at work by helping them identify their most important happiness factors and providing them with the resources that will help them improve in those work-life areas. In doing so, we not only help them become happier and more productive at work, we are helping them become happier in life."

Cheery messaging aside, CareerBliss strives to be a one-stop shop for everything you need to get the best job possible. It provides information about companies, positions, salaries, and user opinions.

For example, the "Reviews" section offers anonymous reviews of companies. Here are a few examples of the over 400 reviews posted about General Electric:

Three stars (out of five): "GE is one of the best places I've worked. If you are technical, you will be challenged every day. Mobility, pay structure, and benefits are a bit antiquated."

Four stars: "My sales experience at GE was very challenging and I gained knowledge of working with many different customers and corporate divisions, which helps strengthen my overall sales ability."

Three stars: "I've worked at GE Oil & Gas for 2+ years. They treat their employees with very little respect. They set impossible deadlines, then ream them when those impossible deadlines are not met. Unless you are in management, you will be treated like a number and not part of a family."

There are additional subcategories that users rank, such as "Way you work" and "Company culture." Overall, GE has done pretty well, with an average review of four out of five stars.

WORKPLACEDYNAMICS

It's a fact of life that forums such as CareerBliss, Glassdoor, and others have become well established in today's activated digital environment. But how reliable are they? Many have questioned whether a voluntary community bulletin board can be truly representative of a company's culture and the attitudes of its employees, past and present. One factor may be the tendency of grumpy employees to vent by posting their complaints, while happy employees simply don't think about doing that.

Founded in 2006, WorkplaceDynamics attempts to police the police. They decided to check on the accuracy of sites including Glassdoor; as WorkplaceDynamics said, "The growing popularity of job review sites like Glassdoor and CareerBliss is causing problems for many companies. We appreciate that these sites are trying to bring more transparency into what it's like to work at a company—but unfortunately these sites are often not an accurate reflection of the workplace."

To test the accuracy of these sites, WorkplaceDynamics compared its data on over four hundred large companies with those same companies' corresponding reviews on Glassdoor. WorkplaceDynamics claimed that the overall Glassdoor star rating was a very poor indicator of what it is really like to work at a company.

Why the disconnect? Two reasons.

▶ Glassdoor typically has reviews from only a small percentage of employees at the company.

▶ Glassdoor reviews tend to be posted by a disproportionate number of unhappy employees. WorkplaceDynamics conservatively estimated that a company's negative employees are up to eight times more likely to post a review on Glassdoor than their positive employees.

These two factors can make the overall Glassdoor scores skewed. They cited as examples the case of Quicken Loans, which WorkplaceDynamics had listed at number one on its National Top Workplaces list.

Quicken Loans is the nation's largest online retail mortgage lender and the second largest overall retail lender in the United States. The company has about ten thousand employees, of which six thousand work at the company headquarters in Detroit, Michigan. For the past ten years, it's been listed as one of the top thirty companies on Fortune magazine's annual "100 Best Companies to Work For" list.

On Glassdoor, Quicken Loans had a mediocre score of 3.2 stars. A whopping 46% of employees would not recommend the company to a friend. Sounds bad, doesn't it? But this result was based on only 140 reviews. In their own survey of Quicken Loans, Workplace Dynamics received 935 survey responses. Of these, only two percent of employees would not recommend the company, with a further five percent being neutral. On average, employees rated working at Quicken loans a 90.3 on a scale of zero to ninety-nine.

So, while the intent of sites like Glassdoor is good, job seekers should think twice before making any decisions based on reviews from these sites when looking for a new employer.

Workplace commentary and ratings are a fact of life. Employees are increasingly willing to reveal their salaries and want to know the salaries of co-workers. What can a company do?

As the Wall Street Journal reported, while companies may not like transparency, under the federal National Labor Relations Act they cannot legally prevent rank-and-file employees from disclosing their pay either internally or externally. That means that an employee handbook or social-media policy barring workers from disclosing their pay is probably a violation of the law. (The rules are different for managers and supervisors, who can legally be prevented from disclosing pay.)

IF YOU CAN'T BEAT 'EM, JOIN 'EM

One way for employers to head off internal politics is to become as transparent as possible.

For example, Buffer is a young company that makes an app that helps users manage multiple social media accounts at once. Users can quickly schedule content from anywhere on the web, collaborate with team members, and analyze rich statistics on how their posts perform.

Leo Widrich, the co-founder of Buffer, told Inc. magazine, "Building Buffer as a 'normal' start-up was never something that excited us. If you go ahead and start your own company, that's finally the chance to really put all your ideas for how great companies are built in practice.... Something that was definitely very scary for us to do was make all salaries public within the company. We created a formula for how salaries are calculated and added it to our Wiki page for everyone on the team to see.

"We wanted to truly commit to our value of transparency. It made hiring new people for our team a lot easier and, yes, you guessed it, more transparent. In fact, we could tell potential employees how much they would earn before we got into any other details. We just ran through the formula and came up with the number."

Launched in 2011 by tech entrepreneur and former Square-space CEO Dane Atkinson, SumAll is a cross-platform marketing analytics company based in New York City. The company's platform combines social media, web traffic, sales metrics and other data to allow customers to track business and social media metrics.

As Atkinson told PBS, "I have on many occasions paid the exact same skill set wildly different fees because I was able to negotiate with one person better than another." Some employees were worth $70,000 a year, but only asked for $50,000 a year. So, he said, he paid them $50,000 a year.

This system works fine until an employee discovers that a co-worker with the same job description is making far more. "I've seen people cry and scream at each other," he told PBS.

When SumAll first started, there were just ten people, and they collectively decided what everyone would be paid. As they kept hiring, Atkinson would say to the new candidate: Here's what everyone gets paid.

Atkinson is happy to explain to an employee why a co-worker makes more, and to explain to that employee how he or she can make more.

Transparency isn't just for Silicon Valley startups. In July 2014, the Philadelphia School District made its salary information available to the general public. The district published the free information, along with OpenDataPhilly, to promote transparency and community engagement. Since the previous year, the district had published ten sets of data, with the salary information being the most recent. The data was provided as a zip file that can be viewed using Excel or other spreadsheet programs.

"We are a public institution," district spokesman Fernando Gallard said in the Philadelphia Daily News. "We are driven to be as transparent as possible, and that has been the way we have operated, and we have provided this information before. Now it's going to be easier."

INSIGHTS: MARK STOUSE, V.P. OF GLOBAL CONNECT AT BMC SOFTWARE

When I first got started in this business a big part of my value was my ability to manage the delta between the *reality* of something and the way the organization wanted that reality to be seen and understood by outside observers. Today, that gap has largely collapsed, and I'm actually very thankful about it. Today, it has never been more important for people in my position to be willing to be the conscience of the organization. To actively say, "These are the choices that we are being presented with and these are the consequences of these choices. What are you prepared to entertain, Mr. CEO?"

This is all part of a technological evolution. Many years ago, I wrote a baccalaureate paper, the thesis of which was this: "What would have happened in the American Civil War if television had been present at the Battle of Gettysburg?" The takeaway there was that the American people on both sides would have risen up and said, "That's it, we're done, and we're going to be two countries for a while," because the losses were so horrific.

You clearly saw that play out in Vietnam, which was the first televised war. Just as TV is a very emotional medium, you could argue that social is even more emotional. It taps into the essence of a person's beliefs because it is bilateral. It's not just a signal coming into them that influences them; they can then go back out.

Benjamin R. Barber, the famous political scientist who back in the early 1980s wrote *Strong Democracy: Participatory Politics for a New Age*, a seminal work on the impact of technology on democracy, could not have really envisioned social back then.

But when you read his book, which has since been updated many times, that's what he's talking about. He's talking about the complete erosion of the monolithic, top-down, command and control version of democracy. All that sounds very disconnected: how can you have command and control in democracy? I think that clearly we have seen that but things are moving apart and I think that you're seeing this in marketing, you're seeing this in coms, you're seeing it in HR, you're seeing it in IT, where people are saying, "We are unwilling to play by the old rules."

A person in my position has to be willing to play a completely different game that is really much more about influencing the people who make the decisions and then facilitating the understanding of those decisions across a broad front with many different audiences.

You can't say one thing to one group but another thing to another group, like you used to twenty years ago. It's possible to emphasize different things to different audiences, but you'd better be reading off the same piece of sheet music.

CHAPTER 14
THE POWER OF GAMIFICATION

One day, Emperor Ceo was strolling along one of his many corridors of power. He was pondering an ancient question that has vexed many a leader: how to get the members of his court to be more engaged. Too many of his princes and dukes were calling in sick instead of going on crusades. Too many vassals and serfs were hanging out by the water cooler—the bubbling spring hidden deep in the royal forest—rather than toiling in the fields.

Paying them more was not always the best solution. Threats didn't seem to work. The high-priced management consultant hired by the emperor had cost a small fortune and had produced no measurable results.

Suddenly the emperor's silent solitude was interrupted by a child's shout.

"Yippeee!"

Emperor Ceo scowled. He spied a page—the same kid who had beat him up in the previous chapter for two gold coins as his fee for running to the deli.

"You—lowly page!" said the emperor. "Why art thou shouting like that? It is most unseemly."

The page looked up from his mobile phone. "Oh—sorry, Your Highness," he said. "I was just playing a game."

"Playing a game?" thundered the emperor. "On court time?

Do I pay you to play games?"

"Well, yes, in fact you do," replied the page. "The duke of HR set it up. It's a court management simulator. I play the part of the royal housekeeper. For every fifty rats that I kill, I move up one level. If I complete all five levels I'll qualify for a promotion to head rat catcher."

"That's a plum assignment," said the emperor.

"You bet. I'll get my own office in the corner tower. Ten junior rat catchers will report to me. It's a sweet gig."

"You say that HR set this up?" inquired the emperor.

"Yeah," said the page. "Staff are playing games all over the castle. People love it. Marketing is getting in on the action, too. They're partnering with an app creator to develop a game where you hunt for a dragon. They think it will drive up enlistment in the knights' training college."

"I could use a few more good knights," mused the emperor.

There's a word for what's happening at the castle—gamification. It's the use of game thinking and game mechanics in non-game contexts to engage users in solving problems. Gamification is being applied in many domains including improving user engagement, physical exercise, return on investment, data quality, timeliness, and learning.

Though the term "gamification" was coined in 2002 by Nick Pelling, a British-born computer programmer and inventor, it took until 2010 to become widespread when referring to incorporation of social/reward aspects of games into software.

Like the page who is rewarded for freeing the castle of rodents, a core gamification strategy is the dispensing of rewards for players who accomplish desired tasks. Types of rewards include points, achievement badges or levels, the filling of a progress bar, providing the user with virtual currency, or even (as we shall see with Kiip) actual goods or services.

In some cases, existing tasks are made to feel more like games. Some techniques used in this approach include adding meaningful choice, onboarding with a tutorial, increasing challenges, and adding narrative.

Competition can be another element of gamification. Making the rewards for accomplishing tasks visible to other players or the posting of leader boards are ways of encouraging players or coworkers to constructively compete.

Customers are not the only constituents of a company who can be made to feel more engaged and motivated. Employees can also benefit significantly from gamification programs that foster an environment in which they feel recognized and rewarded for their achievements. The human resources function of any business can leverage gamification techniques to incent and reward employees for completing key tasks.

GAMIFICATION ON THE JOB

Human resource teams can leverage gamification to achieve several business goals.

ENHANCE TALENT ACQUISITION AND MANAGEMENT

A game experience can support the hiring process by rewarding prospects with both acknowledgement and tangible perks for completing a series of steps, from application to hire. Onboarding efficiency can be enhanced as candidates are motivated to complete various steps to earn rewards. For example, Marriott Hotels launched a mobile app that makes candidates virtually perform hotel service industry tasks. This provides insight into how the candidate would approach real work and it helps eliminate those applicants lacking the patience or aptitude for the job.

Internally, HR teams can also use gamification to reward top recruiters and incentivize employees to refer top candidates.

BUILD CORPORATE CULTURE AND RETAIN KEY EMPLOYEES

Employee retention is important in maintaining valuable personnel assets, preserving institutional knowledge, and cutting down costly turnover. Employees can be rewarded for participating in company-wide volunteer programs, effective team collaboration, or providing process or product improvement suggestions.

MOTIVATE EMPLOYEES TO COMMIT TO TRAINING

Employees are often not interested in mandatory HR training programs such as diversity, harassment, and other compliance programs. Adding a game component to the online learning program can spur action. Employees are far more likely to make it a priority when they earn rewards and recognition for having completed these tasks. HR benefits from increased voluntary employee compliance, without having to pressure employees to complete the programs.

INCENTIVIZE ADMINISTRATIVE REQUIREMENTS

Paperwork is unavoidable in areas such as expense reports and the completion of benefits enrollment forms. Rewarding employees with either peer or management recognition for completing required forms can motivate them to get mundane tasks accomplished.

Programs can be designed to allow team members to recognize one another for contributions made toward a common goal.

As a powerful side benefit, the accumulated data can provide a valuable historic record to reflect employee and organizational knowledge. It's easy to identify employees who have worked with clients in a specific industry, achieved certification in specific skills, or have completed mandatory training programs. All of this combines to create a more efficient, collaborative, productive and upwardly motivated workforce.

Today, many companies provide ready-to-deploy gamification modules. These solutions focus on creating an engaging experience by using badges, points, and leader boards.

Gamification offers new ways to align candidate behavior with organizational goals. Instead of telling an employee that he "did not meet expectations," it may be more effective to point out that he or she "did not clear the second level of the game." Human resource administrators can create transparent leader boards with badges attached to each level, so that each employee knows how he or she is doing in their business unit or geographical region. If an organization has an internal social media portal, the conversations and chit-chat around the game could be packaged to enhance employee engagement at this "virtual water cooler."

New hire programs that are gamified are personalized, engaging, and can express creativity within an organization. Instead of sitting through endless lectures, e-learning modules, or training videos, the new employee can play a game that provides all the information he or she needs and connects them to their peers.

The cases for using gamification are numerous and growing. SAP uses games to educate its employees on sustainability; Unilever applies them to training; Hays deploys them to hire recruiters and the Khan Academy uses it for online education.

Aberdeen Group research published in Motivate, Incent, Compensate, Enable: Sales Performance Management Best Practices (January 2013) validates how top-performing organizations take a "kinder, gentler" path to managing sales teams, who then respond positively with better revenue, quota, and profitability results. This research brief examines a relative newcomer to the sales effectiveness space—gamification—and reveals best practices associated with its use.

According to the Aberdeen survey, organizations with gamification in place improve engagement by 48%, as compared to 28% with those who do not, and improve turnover by 36% as compared to twenty-five percent.

A 2011 report by Gartner, Inc., the leading information technology research and advisory company, states that for a gamified application to truly engage its audience, three key ingredients must be present and correctly positioned: motivation, momentum and meaning (collectively known as "M^3"). "Gamification could become as important as Facebook, eBay or Amazon," said Brian Burke, research vice president at Gartner. "During 2012, twenty percent of Global 2000 organizations will deploy a gamified application. IT leaders must start exploring opportunities to use gamification to increase engagement with customers and employees, with the aim of deploying a gamified application.... Understanding how to apply game mechanics to motivate positive behavioral change is critical to success."

Activated companies that are leveraging gamification take the heart of what makes games so appealing (purpose, challenge, and reward), decode the components that make them work (personalization, rankings, and leaderboards) and apply these elements in a wide variety of imaginative solutions to help enhance customer loyalty, motivate customers to buy, and provide compelling mechanisms for hiring and retaining talent.

INSIGHTS: BRIAN WONG, FOUNDER & CEO AT KIIP

In 2010, at the age of nineteen, Canadian Internet entrepreneur Brian Wong co-founded Kiip, a mobile app rewards platform that lets brands and companies give real-world rewards for in-game achievements.

His success was not surprising. At the age of eighteen, Brian received a degree in Commerce from the University of British Columbia. While at university, he launched his first company, FollowFormation, which Mashable called "the easiest way to follow the top Twitterers by subject matter or topic." Brian also worked for the business development of Digg, leading the development and release of the Digg Android Mobile App.

Among many other honors, at the age of twenty, he was named to the Forbes "30 Under 30" list, and he's been named one of "The Top 5 Young Entrepreneurs to Watch" by Mashable.

His idea for Kiip (pronounced "keep") first came to him on an airplane, when he observed his fellow passengers on their iPads. Many passengers were playing games, and he saw that the games' advertisements were both intrusive and didn't add any real value. Brian realized that a marketer could leverage key moments of game achievement—such as level ups and high scores—with a targeted, relevant physical rewards program that enabled a brand to reach consumers when they were most engaged. Instead of digital rewards, Kiip provides consumers with tangible rewards from premium brands and companies, such as a free bottle of Propel Fitness Water offered by Pepsi inside the Nexercise and Sworkit apps for every eight miles run by a user.

An app becomes "Kiip-enabled" by first deciding which moments deserve to be rewarded in their app. After contacting Kiip, they download and integrate the company's software development kit (SDK or "devkit," which for non-techies is typically a set of software development tools that allows for the creation of applications for a certain software package, software framework, hardware platform, computer system, video game console, operating system, or similar development platform).

The player plays the game app, and when they reach a preset goal or level, the reward pops up. Just as with banners and other traditional forms of mobile advertising, app users can ignore Kiip reward offers when they appear. Kiip only charges advertisers when users actually redeem an offer. According to Xconomy, the company reports that five to seven percent of all offers are redeemed, which is a higher rate than click-throughs on typical mobile banner ads.

Kiip makes redeeming an offer as easy as possible. A gamer who has just leveled up in a game like Unblock Me, for example, might see a reward notification for a free Sour Patch Kids sample. They gamer taps the notification, and gets a message from the brand congratulating them for their achievement and asking for their e-mail address. That prompts an email from Kiip that asks for their shipping address. Other rewards, such as Amazon MP3 credits, are instantly redeemable online.

Kiip makes money by charging brands when a user claims a reward in-app on a cost per engagement basis (CPE). Kiip splits every dollar 50/50 with developers in the network.

As of this writing, Kiip is active on more than a thousand apps played on seventy-five million devices. It gives out eleven rewards per second and sends out reward notices for over 500 million moments monthly.

Kiip is expanding beyond the notoriously volatile game market into more stable mobile fitness apps like MapMyRun, Nexercise, LoloFit, Gym-Pact and others. The company has also integrated with productivity apps, including Any.DO and Finish

2.0, and has integrated with the Yahoo! Japan app, the first time Yahoo! Japan has integrated a third-party service into its app.

To supply rewards, the company has established strategic partnerships with more than 115 major brands, including 7-Eleven, Amazon, American Apparel, Campbell's, Ford, Hasbro, Macy's, McDonald's, Mondelēz International (formerly Kraft Foods), Pepsi, Procter & Gamble, Sony Music, Unilever, Verizon, and Wrigley.

Brian sat down with me and offered his powerful insights into the impact of gaming and digital communications on every facet of business.

In Brian's view, too many brands are still communicating through old methods and old measurements to define those methods when it comes to anything digital. And right now, the way that many brands are connecting and communicating their messages is primarily through disruptive and annoying tactics, whether it be banner ads, full-screen ads, or video ads. Typically, when you're in the middle of doing something you pretty much only accidentally tell them anything, such as accidently clicking on something.

Brian and his team realized that this was a big problem, and so the inspiration came from looking at what he calls "moments of achievement" in the apps and links that people use every single day. He wanted to tap into the existing patterns of behavior rather than make new ones. The existing patterns of behavior he saw were ready to be leveraged. Whether it be leveling up in a game, logging a run in your running app, or finishing off a Sudoku, those are all existing patterns of behavior that encompass emotion. You're actually feeling something such as feeling happy when you run. In that moment you should be acknowledged, otherwise it's a serendipitous acknowledgment.

They ended up building a tech that would be better than all the things people happen to be doing already. Let's say you've already run; you could be rewarded with a bottle of Gatorade. That would just be one very small example of many things that they're doing to try to change the way the brand is seen and how they communicate with people.

The ad is so personal that there's no excuse not to be conscious of the contacts of what you're doing and actually adding value instead of taking away and being an obscure nuisance.

There are many existing norms that marketers are still comfortable doing, such as using the frequency method of communicating with people, which he knew was an ultimate flaw. Just because you showed something to a consumer a hundred times doesn't mean that he or she wants to buy it more, it just means that it happens to be there a hundred times. That's the thing he realized wasn't going to work on a mobile contact. When it came to actually doing something different it wasn't that hard, it was just almost pretending you didn't know anything about the old world, and Brian thinks that's something that helps significantly when it comes to disruption and being inspired. It's about, "What if I didn't know that the banner ad ever existed? What if we lived in a world where the banner ad hadn't even been invented? What does that mean, and how do we use that as a starting point?"

The good news is that there are many digital natives who are very astute at ignoring these things, and so there is a world for many people where that doesn't even exist. So the only way that a brand can be there is by doing the exact opposite of advertising. After all, traditional advertising is taking and taking and taking. It's always been about taking your time, taking your attention and taking your space. Kiip flips over that equation and turns it around; it looks at giving and rewarding and being a part of what you're doing already. That's basically it.

If you look at twenty-year-olds, thirty-year-olds, and fifty-year-olds, you'll see that the way they communicate, the simplest things, are completely different. It's about text versus using their voicemail or using their corporate Internet or any of the opportunities to just send a message to each other; encode and decode.

Like Snapchat, for example. As much as people like to make fun of it, Snapchat is a representation of a morality and instant gratification. The lightness of connection between the two parties involved. When you look at the means of digital communication, before, writing a letter had a little wait to it. But now because it's much quicker, it's about in the moment. We live in moments, and it's about being able to showcase those moments in the most representational way of how we want to receive those messages. And right now it is through something that is quick, and there's that fun in decoding and encoding it, and that is the generation that we live in.

There's a way of communicating in the workplace that people will find the most productive for the type of business that they're in. Brian thinks we are so hung up on telecommuting and other methods like intranets and yammer style communication and that different companies will have different characteristics they will use to communicate better.

For example, says Brian, "We have offices in San Francisco, New York City, Los Angeles, Chicago, Vancouver, London, Bogota and Tokyo. To communicate we try everything from cameras that people can walk up to the screen and tap on and say hi to other people, to FaceTime, to Skype; and literally the best method that we've all resorted to is picking up the phone and calling them on their cell phone. We've opted as a company, for example, not to have Polycom. We have Polycoms in the conference room, but I'm talking about the polycom sitting on your desk having your own phone, a landline. That just isn't how we do it. There's a lot of IM-ing. We have a lot of chitchat going on and it's just how we run the company, so it's not a generational thing."

What we're forgetting is that we're all the same generation now. It's a connected generation. One thing that will be common across all employees eventually is we'll all hold a smartphone, and the way we communicate will be representative of how connected we are. You're seeing also that fascinating dynamic of the consumerization of the enterprise, which means essentially fewer people holding Blackberries and more people holding iPhones with corporate. You would have your work phone and you would always bash it and say, "This was provided by work," but now there's a desire to bring in your phone and your own computer. It's happening more and more, and that's allowing people to have fun with it in the communication styles. The tools to communicate are different as well. It's starting to move in the right direction and to be a lot more uniform than it used to be. It's about the type of organization you are, not about who comprises that organization.

Culture plays a role in what works and what doesn't, whether it's marketing automation or CRM, or even implementing social media applications in companies; and the biggest challenge that we're seeing as a trend is the problem with user adaption. When you ask the question obviously it comes down to the culture of communication within that company.

Companies are becoming more and more visional. The fundamental movement is that you're going to rely a lot more on digital channels for sales and customer communication, and that'll eventually lead to the employees themselves and how they adapt to it. A lot of CPGs and retailers are selling more and more online, and more and more of their customers are going to communicate to them via social media. If they cannot survive in that environment, their company won't survive. A lot of this is pure survival, and that's why we're seeing this movement and why it's happening so quickly.

When you've been around for a hundred years, how do you get people excited about what you're doing? That's a big issue.

One of the things Brian has seen is that communicating the "why" over the "what" is much more important these days for not only recruiting but creating an interior communication culture that has people aiming for the right thing. It's really easy to describe what you do—"I'm doing this, I'm doing that, this stuff has functions, this stuff has bells and whistles," but why you're doing it is a much more powerful position to explain and to guide people towards. It will ultimately be a lot more directional than purely a plan of attack and what needs to be done and then to do it.

Coming from new generations of companies that are based on massive visions and connecting people, it's not about the fact that it's got a chat function and you can add friends and creep on their photos. You've got to add the "why," which is re-organizing the world's information.

A lot of companies are forgetting that in the old days of making widgets, it was about what you're making, and you're making it cheaper and it's going to be in a factory and it's going to have people that have been there for a hundred years. But the days of that are now fading quickly. It's about who can be differentiated in their vision. The "what" is less important now, because if someone wants to go ahead and outsource the creation of a production line of a product that they want to build, that doesn't take a lot of time now. It's not about needing to set up a factory relationship and them taking an extra million-dollar bone, it may just be going after a company in China that can build it for you and getting it done that way.

Ultimately it's the marketing of your product that will get people excited and on board with you.

Of the companies that exist today and that we think of as constants, who do you think is going to go out of business? With all due respect to the Twitters of the world and Google, if you have to think ten years down the road, there are so many competing communication technologies and platforms, do you envision in ten years some kind of consolidation where everything is provided through a single thread, or do you envision that what used to be taking a decade and which is now happening in six months is going to even further be compressed in terms of changes in communications in what we do?

Communication is going to be a lot more fragmented. You look at a hundred years ago versus now, and we have so many more options. There really was never a cycle of consolidation like the telephone. While in many ways the telephone was a consolidation of multiple telephones and standards, the whole idea of putting an earpiece up to your ear and another piece to your mouth remained. So the companies that'll survive are the ones that have those ingredients and know how to leverage it and to put it into a communication protocol. One hundred and forty characters has a different social setting which is acceptable and has different use cases to it. A lot of it is breaking news, a lot of it is personal opinions and a lot of it is brevity for the sake of brevity. If Twitter's smart enough to make themselves the backbone of technology, where you can build other communication styles off of their platform, it's important. The more closed off they are, the more difficult that may become. For you to look at your crystal ball, a lot of it is going to be who's going to be like the telecoms of the early century and who can then be the consolidating force that brings all of them together under the same common use case. That's what's going to end up happening.

A CEO of the new generation needs to think "SMS." It's back to basics. Each communication method will have its own purpose, so if you're calling your boss and it's important, it will require his or her full and undivided attention and real-time response. Translation: If you're emailing the young CEO, you may not get an answer until the next day. That's the priority with which this executive likes to set as his communications protocol with his team. If you don't get it or your people don't get it, imagine the innate gap in productivity and expectations.

The old days of your secretary picking up the phone for you and printing out emails so you can read them are over. It's not that hard to get these things and, the fact that anybody of any age can pick up an iPhone and an iPad and figure it out is a testament to Apple's ability to make technology seamless for all. At the same time it's tide after tide; people need to be able to get this stuff and if they can't they're going to die out.

In the old days you could say, "What's this technology? It doesn't really matter because it doesn't seem like it's got a big impact," but the world is operating on an entirely new language today, and we have English and then we have code and you've got to understand how code works or at least interacts with something else. If you don't, you're going to be gone.

CHAPTER 15
MEASURE SUCCESS OR ELSE

Be honest: when was the last time corporate management said **"I LOVE the engagement return-on-investment! This really helped us GROW this quarter!"** If you're being honest with yourself, chances are the answer is slim to none. The majority of us never experienced *joy* when it comes to explaining digital engagement ROI to a corporate non-marketer like a CEO, CFO or CIO (unless of course they are in marketing automation or run a social media startup). It seems that measuring digital marketing, and social media ROI seems to be as elusive today as ever.

Reality bites: Why is it that with the amount of Big Data analytics and KPIs that are now readily available to us, we still don't seem to get it right? I often envision that if Digital Marketing ROI was a perfume, it would be branded as **"Frustration"** by Calvin Klein.

Yet surprisingly, most of us do little critical thinking but tend to have a lot of ready-made answers that mostly end with "it's not our fault". In other words, we don't seem to ask the right questions. In comes the highly effective Socratic Method. Yes, Socrates, that old Greek philosopher dude, had a pretty cool method of getting to the heart of the problem.

Think your colleagues don't appreciate your digital ROI? Maybe you should start by challenging the commonly held truths and fallacies about marketing ROI and digital specifically! Consider examining your digital and social media ROI metrics against the following digital Socratic questions and see if they hold water. At worst, you will become a digital philosopher with more followers than Socrates. At best, you'd become the digital leader that your company deserves.

▶ **Are you focused on digital marketing ROI or Business outcomes?** Big data analytics allow us to measure digital engagement, influence, velocity, frequency and repeat visits and downloads. But do any of these measurements matter when it comes to sales, marketing or public relations? Align the metrics you measure with the ones that the CFO, CIO and CEO are using like cash flow, contribution to revenue, creation of new profit centers or reduction in overhead by using innovation communications.

▶ **Do I have the 'Buy-In' from non-marketing stakeholders to marketing automation as a revenue enhancer?** The fact that you embraced digital marketing, marketing automation and social media doesn't mean that leadership understands the 'why' behind the 'how.' They might consider it to be another IT infrastructure expense rather than the insightful tool that it could be to double sales. When rolling out a new program, make sure that the buy-in isn't limited to the marketing and public relations teams.

▶ **Do I have the reporting platform to keep the C-Suite engaged?** Nothing could more frustrating than having a big win in social media engagement than having your boss say 'so what, that's not our target audience, irrelevant'. It happens because successful communications cannot be a cartoony dashboard in the boardroom. Take the initiative and interview your boss about what she cares about, then leverage the relationship to build a position where you can report the outcomes of your great successes and learning data in front of the decision makers.

You see; the word *'engagement'* applies not only to the external target audience but also to your leadership, which enables you to make digital marketing success a monetized experience and a promotable career, with tangible results.

Activate, measure, refine and measure again. That's what it takes to Power Up Your Brand, Dominate Your Market, Crush Your Competition & Win In The Digital Age.

SOURCES:

Chapter 1:

▶ The Nielsen Company, "State of the Media: Social Media Report," 2011.

▶ Direct Marketing News, "Mobile Marketing By the Numbers," 2014.

▶ Cloud Driven Limited, "Driving the People Business-How Gamification Creates Sustainable Competitive Advantage for Your Business," July 2014.

Chapter 2:

▶ The Nielsen Company, "State of the Media: Social Media Report," 2011.

▶ Content Marketing Institute/MarketingProfs. "B2B Content Marketing: 2014 Benchmarks, Budgets, and Trends," 2013.

▶ Barry, Chris, Rob Markey, Eric Almquist, and Chris Brahm. "Putting Social Media to Work," *Bain & Company,* September 12, 2011.

Chapter 3:

▶ Pinder, Aly. "M2M and Business Analytics: Driving the Smarter Machine to the Internet of Things." *The Aberdeen Group, August 8, 2013.*

▶ Econsultancy, 2014 Digital Trends, January, 2014, P. 6, From Econsultancy Website.

▶ Chadwick Martin Bailey, "10 Facts about Consumer Behavior on Twitter," 2012.

Chapter 4:

▶ Keenan, Jim, and Barbara Giamanco. "Social Media and Sales Quota," *A Sales Guy Consulting,* 2014.

▶ ExactTarget Marketing Cloud, "2014 State of Marketing," *Sales Force Exacttarget,* 2014.

Chapter 5:

▶ Alterra Group, "Account-Based Marketing: An Approach on the Rise," 2014.

▶ Lattice, "Decoding Predictive Marketing," June 23, 2014.

▶ Munchbach, Cory, Tracy Stokes, Lucas Paderni, and Alexandra Hayes. "The Role of Digital in the Path to Purchase," *Forrester Research, Inc.,* August 27, 2012.

Chapter 6:

▶ Pew Research Center. "Millenials in Adulthood," March 7, 2014.

▶ Pew Research Center. February, May, August, 2013.

▶ BazaarVoice. "Talking to Strangers: Millenials Trust People over Brands," January, 2012.

Chapter 7:

▶ Edelman/Strategy One, "The 8095 Exchange: Millennials, Their Actions Surrounding Brands, and the Dynamics of Reverberation," October, 2010.

▶ ExactTarget Marketing Cloud, "2014 State of Marketing," Sales Force Exacttarget, 2014.

▶ Yankee 451 Group. "Mobile Money: The Exploding New Opportunity," November, 2012.

Chapter 8:

▶ Act-on Software. "Fast Facts," 2014.

▶ Cisco Visual Networking Index. May, 2014

▶ Lattice. "Decoding Predictive Marketing," June 23, 2014.

Chapter 9:

▶ Lattice. "Decoding Predictive Marketing," June 23, 2014.

CPSIA information can be obtained at www.ICGtesting.com
Printed in the USA
BVOW05*1235280814

364372BV00001B/3/P